AF708412

Integrity First

Reflections of a Military Philosopher

Malham M. Wakin

LEXINGTON BOOKS
Lanham • Boulder • New York • Oxford

LEXINGTON BOOKS

Published in the United States of America
by Lexington Books
4720 Boston Way, Lanham, Maryland 20706

12 Hid's Copse Road
Cumnor Hill, Oxford OX2 9JJ, England

Copyright © 2000 by Lexington Books

All rights reserved. No part of this publication may be reproduced, stored in a retrieval system, or transmitted in any form or by any means, electronic, mechanical, photocopying, recording, or otherwise, without the prior permission of the publisher.

British Library Cataloguing in Publication Information Available

Library of Congress Cataloging-in-Publication Data

Wakin, Malham M.
Integrity first : reflections of a military philosopher / Malham M. Wakin.
p. cm.
ISBN 0-7391-0170-6 (cloth : alk. paper)
1. Military ethics. 2. Military ethics—United States. 3. War—Moral and ethical aspects. I. Title.

U22 .W27 2000
172'.42—dc21 00-042124

Printed in the United States of America

™ The paper used in this publication meets the minimum requirements of American National Standard for Information Sciences—Permanence of Paper for Printed Library Materials, ANSI/NISO Z39.48–1992.

To Marion, Sue, and Bertha, three wonderful, dedicated teachers whose lives were cut short by personal tragedies.

CONTENTS

Introduction ix

I. In the Beginning 1
1 Dynamism and Discipline 3

II. Essays of General Interest 11
2 On the Nature of Man 13
3 Egoism, Greed, and America's Future 33
4 Egoism as a Moral Theory 39

III. Ethics and the Military Profession 51
5 The Vocation of Arms 53
6 The American Military: Theirs to Reason Why 61
7 The Ethics of Leadership I 69
8 The Ethics of Leadership II 87
9 The Military: A Noble Profession 103
10 Wanted: Moral Virtues in the Military 109
11 Professional Integrity 113

IV. Warfare: Moral Issues 121
12 Morality and War 123
13 God or Guns: A False Dichotomy 133
14 Just War, Nuclear Deterrence, and the Strategic Defense Initiative 143
15 Applying Nuremberg Principles to Limited War 149
16 Humanitarian Intervention : An Idea Whose Time Has Come 157

V. Do We Know What We're Doing? 161
17 Military and Societal Values: The Relevance of Knowing and Doing 163
18 Technology and Education: A Philosopher's Perspective 169

VI. And in the End 177
19 Teaching Philosophy at the United States Air Force Academy 179

About the Author 183

INTRODUCTION

I have put these papers together with a bit of uneasiness. Is anyone interested in the kinds of things a professional military officer who teaches philosophy at the Air Force Academy might think about? Somehow, I have persuaded myself that others, perhaps most citizens of a democracy, ought to have some concern for the kind of thinking and teaching that goes on at our military academies. Over the past forty years I have tried very hard to present courses that would cause our potential officers to become better thinkers, value-conscious leaders, and morally sensitive decision-makers. In this same period of time I have lectured extensively at institutions throughout the United States, briefly in Europe, and frequently in Canada. The papers I've included here are a representative sampling of the kinds of issues about which both military and civilian audiences have inquired. I hope you'll find here some rather plain thinking that strives to achieve a sense of balance and is marked throughout with a decent smattering of common sense.

A word of explanation is in order about gender references: some of these papers were written when the Air Force Academy was an all-male institution and since they were published previously in various places, I have not rewritten them to reflect the current coeducational status of our student body.

Part I

IN THE BEGINNING

Chapter 1

DYNAMISM AND DISCIPLINE:

The Role of Philosophy at the United States Air Force Academy

"The professional military mind is by necessity an inferior and unimaginative mind; no man of high intellectual quality would willingly imprison his gifts in such a calling." – H.G. Wells, *Outline of History*

The quotation above expresses quite forcefully a conception of the "military mind" which can be found in many literary characterizations of the military officer, some fictional and some nonfictional. Additional descriptions of such a mind find it to be conservative, disciplined, unconcerned, uninformed, and, surprisingly enough, morally insensitive. The last characteristic is attributed to the "garrison mind" by Murray Kempton, who states that "the good soldier will lie under orders as bravely as he will die under them. The garrison mind can produce acts that are honorable and even gallant; but notions of high virtue and selfless service seldom intrude upon it, being disposed of by discipline."[1]

I have pointed out this particular and perhaps popularized view of the intellectual and moral abilities and attitudes of military officers since it is clear that the institutional goal of the Air Force Academy is directly opposed to the production and preservation of officers who fit the "military mind" stereotype. It has seemed to me particularly paradoxical that the attitude which creates the stereotype described above must assume that the qualities of obedience and loyalty which we esteem greatly in young people, particularly in our own children when they are ascribed to career military officers, are assumed to be in some sense necessarily conjoined to stupidity and moral laxity. The villain in the case seems to be discipline. If I analyze the deprecating attitudes correctly, they hold that, in brief, discipline and dynamism do not mix; a mind which readily and habitually obeys orders can hardly be thought to be either brilliant or creative. The aim of the Air Force Academy, as I conceive it, stands in sharp contradistinction to the previously described view; we hope to graduate dedicated officers who are intellectually gifted, broadly educated, morally resolute, and capable of mature leadership under the most trying conditions.

This chapter first appeared in *The New Scholasticism*, 41 (summer 1967), 336-66. The update (1979) and the article were published in *The First Twenty-Five Years*, USAF Academy, 1979, 173-185. Reprinted with permission.

What kind of a curriculum can satisfy that aim? What should be the role of philosophy in an institution where it is held that military leaders can and ought to be thinkers as well as doers? As a former dean of the faculty at the Air Force Academy[2] has pointed out, there are two major functions which the curriculum must serve. It must offer those courses which our students should study because they are, first of all, men. These courses should be in the liberal arts and sciences; this portion of the curriculum should insure a broad and liberal education. The second function which the curriculum should accomplish concerns the unique professional mission of a military academy; it should provide a number of courses which a student should study because he is going to be a professional military man. Literature, law, physics, and philosophy all fall in the category of those courses which a man studies because he is a man; aeronautics, astronautics, electrical engineering, military history, and other more specific military training courses fall into the professional category.

It is worth mentioning here that military decisions in our time cannot be made in isolated fashion. Military leaders must act from a fundamental knowledge of the political, economic, religious, and, yes, philosophical implications of their decisions. It is unthinkable that military problems in Vietnam today can be considered completely apart from the religious, cultural, and philosophical traditions of the Vietnamese. To attempt to find solutions to problems in Southeast Asia today without first attempting to understand Buddhism, Communism, and the relevance of Western value systems is to prejudice in advance any possibility of even a semipermanent settlement of the unrest in that part of the world. This is not to say that every military leader must be a philosopher; what I am trying to point out is that he must be a student of philosophy in the sense that he, first of all, understands and, second, does not ignore philosophical positions, both those of his friends and those of his enemies. There is a great deal of relevance in G.K. Chesterton's comment: "We think that for a general about to fight an enemy, it is important to know the enemy's numbers, but still more important to know the enemy's philosophy."[3]

Not too long ago, a visiting colleague suggested that it seemed rather a mistake to teach philosophy to cadets since inculcation of philosophic attitudes would naturally result in their questioning policies, deliberating over the appropriateness of obeying certain orders, etc. Philosophy would seem to produce more Hamlets than command decision heroes. He suggested that if our students reflect philosophically about their own situations too long we will either have poor soldiers or we will lose them to other professions. This suggestion ought not be ignored; it quite obviously relates to our earlier references to the "military mind."

Taking our cue from Socrates' dictum that "the unexamined life is not worth living" (hence, we ought to examine our lives), we might say in parallel fashion, "the unexamined ideal is not worth dying for." Since examining ideals is usually considered the business of the philosophers, and since our students at the Academy have taken a rather serious oath to risk their lives for certain ideals, it is difficult to avoid the conclusion that they should do some philosophy. If after examination of those ideals a cadet decides that they are not worth the risk, then we will indeed lose a potential officer—and we should. Fools alone die for nothing; rational men should be able to justify both living and dying.

Valuations of the worth of professions must take into account the essential function of the profession being examined. Our high regard for the medical profession, for example, stems from its basic function to preserve life; life itself is very high on the scale of human values. Our high regard for judges stems from their essential concern with justice, another important human value. If we are to evaluate the military profession in an analogous way we must decide on its essential function. If we can agree that the function of the military establishment of a free nation is to preserve and protect the way of life of that nation, and if we can agree that the way of life is an important human value, "We must value most, not living, but living well" (Socrates, once again), then it surely follows that the military profession is a noble profession indeed. If we are afraid that exposure to philosophy will turn our students against the military profession then, once more, we must take the risk. It is better to have men in this profession who have rationally evaluated their essential function and decided in its favor than to have an uncommitted corps of officers who might not consider the value commitment involved until that crucial moment of decision which could spell disaster for our nation or even for the human race.

The original planners of the Academy curriculum had included two courses in philosophy, which every student would be required to take. That original curriculum was totally prescribed for four years. During the freshman year each cadet was to take a basic course in logic; during the junior year it was proposed that each cadet take a course in value theory. The total prescribed curriculum at that time was equally divided between the humanities and social sciences on the one hand and the basic and engineering sciences on the other. Actually, by the time the first class at the Academy, the Class of 1959, reached the junior year, revisions in the curriculum had reduced the number of prescribed philosophy courses to one. Curriculum planners at that time decided that there should be one required course which would serve as an introduction to a number of philosophic problems rather than be restricted to one field in philosophy. From 1959 through 1961 every junior took a course designed around original readings which encompassed a number of metaphysical, epistemological, ethical, and sociopolitical problems. At the same time an elective course in ethics became very popular. From 1962 through 1964 each student was able to fulfill the philosophy requirement by electing one of three basic courses, in logic, ethics, or philosophic problems.

These changes in required philosophy offerings were developing along with a gradually evolving overall curriculum. By taking a number of enrichment courses, some advanced students could complete a major in one of four fields: humanities, public affairs, engineering science, and basic science. As more majors were developed, these evolving changes culminated in 1964 in a shift to a curriculum which provided a major for each student within the normal number of semester hours required for graduation. Majors are now available in twenty-seven different fields ranging from humanities to computer science. The concept of a fundamental core curriculum composed of liberal and professional courses has been retained, however. Two-thirds of the approximate total of the forty-nine courses required for graduation remain in the core curriculum which continues to maintain the humanities-social science and basic-engineering science balance.

With the majors-for-all innovation came the obvious problem of replacing one-third of the required courses with courses in the specialized majors. The philosophy requirement was one of the courses which the science and engineering division were unable to include within the scope of their technical majors. All of the majors in the social sciences have included the ethics course as a requirement and each major offered by the humanities division included two philosophy courses. A number of science and engineering students, however, have elected to take courses in the philosophy of science, in ethics, or in comparative religion.

The philosophy function at the Academy has quite clearly been a "service" function in the sense that large numbers of students receive some exposure to philosophy, but there has been no attempt to offer a complete major in philosophy. It is not surprising that courses in ethics and comparative religion should continue to be extremely popular in an institution which must be concerned as much with the development of character as it is with the development of intellect. Explicit recognition of the importance of philosophy in this curriculum was solidified with the appointment of a permanent professor of philosophy in 1964. From the beginning of the institution in 1955, the philosophers assigned to the faculty have been subsidiary members of larger departments; since 1958 the philosophy staff has been attached to the English Department. As a further indication of the institution's recognition of the essential role which philosophy can continue to play in the education of future Air Force leaders, an independent department of philosophy and fine arts will be established during the summer of 1967. A very recent curriculum change approved by the Academy Curriculum Committee and the Academy Board incorporates a prescribed one-semester hour introductory course in philosophy in the unique January term for all sophomores, once more assuring that every student will have at least one direct contact with a formal philosophy course.

These latest curriculum innovations present added challenges to the five members of the current philosophy staff. Our function must continue to be one of support for a number of majors. The computer science majors will take symbolic logic from the philosophy staff; the area studies majors will take our offering in comparative religion; a large number of the majors in social science and humanities fields will continue to take the ethics course; American studies majors must have a course in American philosophy; humanities majors are now required to take three courses in philosophy; the philosophy of science course should still appeal to many science and engineering majors. The greatest challenge, however, will be the introductory course for all sophomores which will be taught for the first time in January 1968. Initial plans for this course are to develop considerations of three basic themes: the nature of man, the nature of human knowledge, and the nature of reality. The major task, of course, consists in showing the relevance of these classical areas of philosophical investigation to today's students and today's problems. It is a rather large order to expect to generate enthusiasm for philosophy and to develop philosophical attitudes through a one-semester-hour course with approximately sixteen meetings, but this is precisely the challenge we face. Interest generated in this course will influence the enrollments in the courses taught during the normal fall and spring semesters. More importantly, the philosophic attitudes generated in this and the other philosophy courses, should assist each student to come to grips with the human predicament in general and his immediate personal involvements in the military in particular.

A word about the student population and teaching conditions at the Air Force Academy may clarify further the impact which enthusiastic philosophers can have in this institution. All of our students are on full four-year scholarships with additional monthly pay, and they are highly selected. The majority of them are eager to tackle philosophical issues and bring with them the broad experiences provided by our balanced core curriculum. During the normal fall and spring semester courses, our class size averages fifteen students, which makes the seminar discussion approach the most popular teaching method. Those instructors with a penchant for the Socratic method find our class situation ideal. Our faculty is all military; every officer who teaches at the Academy has an advanced degree in his field; and 28 percent of the faculty have Ph.D.s. Because our faculty members are officers as well as teachers, they teach by example as well as by lecture. Wearing the uniform enforces the obligation to motivate as well as to educate our student body. We cannot assume responsibility for intellectual development alone but must be continually concerned with character development as well. The existence of this corps of highly educated officers with varied military experience is one piece of evidence that the goal of marrying dynamism with discipline is not altogether ethereal. While our student body can properly be described as exciting, it is not inappropriate to describe our faculty as dynamic and interested: interested in subject matter and most emphatically interested in students.

In this fresh academic atmosphere where the curriculum attempts to incorporate the wisdom of our classical tradition with the latest advances in astronautics and computer science, the philosopher can play both a stabilizing and connecting role. In the fields of ethics and epistemology he serves as a stabilizing influence, calling attention to our moral traditions and forcing rational evaluation of those principles which wearers of the uniform have sworn to defend. In symbolic logic and the philosophy of science he serves as a bridge connecting the humanities division with the science and engineering divisions. Our philosophers have engaged in these and other functions in a number of ways beyond the normal classroom participation. During the summer we have given brief series of lectures on character development to incoming freshmen. Almost every student-faculty discussion group includes a member of our philosophy staff. Subjects discussed in these sessions have ranged from an examination of the conditions for a "just" war to birth control and current sexual mores. Our philosophers are invited very frequently to present informal papers to the separate cadet squadrons and to the various student organizations which include the math club, the student forum, etc. For a number of years our philosophy staff members have functioned as advisors to the student honor and ethics committees. Our student-oriented approach leads naturally to the sort of relationship that results in many informal discussions with students in our professors' homes.

The courses which are currently offered by the philosophy staff include the introductory course for all sophomores in the January term, ethics, comparative religion, philosophical analysis, philosophy of science, American philosophy, introduction to symbolic logic, and an independent study course for seniors. All of the courses except the independent study course and the required sophomore course are taught in small sections of approximately fifteen students each. This means that our instructors teach more often than philosophy instructors at most civilian institutions but our total student load would not be considered excessive. We expect to continue the small-section-discussion approach during the normal fall and spring semesters, but the January term course for approximately one thousand sophomores will have to be taught in large lecture sections. Since this is the one course which provides our philosophers contact with our entire student population, it looms as a most significant challenge.

The role of philosophy in a federal educational institution whose primary goal is to graduate commissioned officers motivated for a lifetime career of service is more complex than the role of philosophy in other colleges and universities. As philosophy professors we share a number of common functions with our colleagues in civilian institutions: we attempt to "humanize" our more technical faculty departments; we hope to stimulate a love for philosophy and significant philosophic problems in our students; we strive to inculcate philosophic attitudes, to encourage serious and rational considerations of issues with ramifications for personal, social, economic, and political life. Our function must be similar to the function of philosophy in other colleges since all of us must deal with the important problems which all students must come to grips with simply because they are human beings. We must foster that natural inclination to "wonder" concerning the nature of reality, the human condition, and the limits of human knowledge. Our function differs from that of our colleagues in other colleges in that we do not plan to graduate students with an extensive major in philosophy. Along with the history, English, and foreign language departments, philosophy and fine arts share the responsibilities of the humanities division for maintaining the strong humanities portion of our curriculum. Majors offered by this division include humanities, history, general studies, military art and science, and American studies. A student with special interests in philosophy could take from two to eight philosophy courses in some of these majors offered by the humanities division.

Additionally, the function of philosophy in the Academy curriculum is particularly significant because of our necessary concern for values and character development. The natural interests of our students in flying and hence in aeronautics and astronautics could have focused our curriculum in strictly technical directions. Philosophy can continue to assist in providing the balanced background which intelligent leaders must have if our way of life is to survive. The picture of philosophy in our time at the Air Force Academy seems quite the reverse of that painted by Aristophanes, who viewed philosophers as men with their heads in the clouds; it is precisely those men who expect to explore beyond the clouds whose attention must be guided to the earthy conditions of human existence by philosophy.

I do not think that it is impossible to attain our idealistic goal of finding in the same men the love of wisdom, ability to accept leadership responsibility, and dedication to country. The student body which comes to us at the Air Force Academy arrives with exceptional potential; philosophy can do much toward developing that potential for intellectual and moral leadership. Because our world and our nation need men of "high intellectual quality" serving as our military leaders, philosophy has an important role to play in this curriculum. If we are to leave the military calling to men with "inferior and unimaginative" minds we must be prepared to accept the consequences of inferior and unimaginative military decisions. The hope for our continuing existence as a free nation or even as a human race could well rest on the possibility of marrying dynamism and discipline.

Update, 1979

In the twelve years since "Dynamism and Discipline" was written, the philosophy program has evolved considerably with even more emphasis being placed on courses in ethics. The short, winter-term introductory course required of all sophomores was taught only for two years (1968 and 1969) under large lecture hall conditions. By 1970 it was scheduled as a half-semester course in small sections for all sophomores, while seniors additionally were able to fill a core option with either the ethics course or a world literature course. The issues raised by the Vietnam War and the Watergate Affair created significant interest in professional ethics and questions related to morality and war. With a major overall shift in the Academy curriculum resulting from the intensive study of the Twentieth Anniversary Curriculum Review Committee, in 1976 the ethics course became the required philosophy course, offered in the junior year.

The number of philosophy instructors is currently stabilized at ten. For the 1977-1978 academic year, the department enjoyed the services of a Distinguished Visiting Professor (Professor Robert Cunningham from San Francisco State University). Upper-division course enrollments, apart from the required ethics course, have declined markedly since 1976 due to the previously mentioned change in the overall curriculum. That change brought about a sharp reduction in the number of free electives available in any student's schedule.

The administrative structure of the department has fluctuated independently of the curriculum offerings. Philosophy was offered by the Department of Philosophy and Fine Arts from 1967 through 1973. An administrative reorganization in 1973 incorporated the fine arts offerings and instructors into the English Department (Department of English and Fine Arts) and combined the personnel and offerings of philosophy and political science (Department of Political Science and Philosophy). In 1977 this administrative action was reversed, and the Department of Philosophy and Fine Arts was reconstituted as a separate entity which is operating currently.

Ethics has become a central focus of the philosophy staff in recent years. Philosophy faculty members have published a number of articles on professional ethics and have been treated as a resource by other service schools, where they have served as curriculum consultants and guest lecturers. Perhaps the most significant publication of department members is the anthology, *War, Morality, and the Military Profession*, which was printed locally in 1978 and will appear in a commercial edition in the summer of 1979. The philosophy program at the Academy seems at this point well established in its continuing function of humanizing the curriculum and focusing the attention of present and future military leaders on the serious ethical dimensions of the military profession.

Notes

1. M. Kempton, "Ribbons and Bibbons," *The New Republic* (November 30, 1963), 14.

2. Brigadier General Robert F. McDermott, to whom goes much of the credit for the early directions of the academic curriculum. General McDermott pioneered such innovations in military education as the enrichment program, cooperative graduate programs, majors for all students, and a "whole man" selection process for incoming candidates.

3. G.K. Chesterton, *Heretics* (Freeport, N.Y.: Books for Libraries Press, 1970), 15.

Part II

ESSAYS OF GENERAL INTEREST

Chapter 2

ON THE NATURE OF MAN

What we think of human nature has a great deal to do with how we behave toward other human beings and indeed with how we treat ourselves. Our views of mankind have made all the difference in our selections of various forms of government, in the kinds of constitutions that have been written, in the wars that we have fought, in our relationships with other kinds of beings like animals, and in our relationships with our environment and our gods. Hence, as you begin a curriculum of studies that encompasses man's institutions, that deals with international politics, and war and peace, it seems appropriate to pause at the outset to review those perspectives on the nature of man that have led us to behave as we do.

I plan to survey briefly a number of influential views of human nature including the metaphysical view of man from the ancients of the far east; the classical Greek views best known to us in the Western world and which have been most influential in Western religions; some quick glimpses of man as seen through the eyes of such thinkers as Thomas Hobbes, John Locke, Immanuel Kant, Karl Marx, Friedrich Nietzsche, and the contemporary existentialists. One caution we must observe regarding these views is that most are extremely complex and have had a variety of expressions over the centuries, but we must of necessity simplify and abbreviate them if we are to discuss them meaningfully in our time together. So, I ask at the outset your kind indulgence if I seem to abridge these positions too severely.

The ancient Eastern view of man contained in the teachings of the philosophical Hindu, the Buddhist, and Chinese Taoism is worth a bit of our time if for no other reason than the fact that it is currently receiving considerable attention on our continent through the efforts of a large number of "missionary" groups. In addition, it seems likely that acquaintance with a culture's prevailing view of human existence may well provide some insight into the appeal which contemporary Marxism-Leninism might have for that people or the resistance which it might meet.

The ancient Hindu view of man is essentially a view which places complete emphasis on the spiritual or inner life and denigrates the external, impermanent, material world. Man is viewed as a being who may be born

---

This chapter was originally developed for presentation at the Inter-American Defense College in the late 1970s and early 1980s. Variations were presented elsewhere in recent years.

many, many times until he escapes the wheel of life by a final permanent union of his atman (individual soul) with the Brahman (the underlying spiritual source of reality). This union is brought about by an intuitive spiritual grasping, a total understanding of the divine Brahman, a total emptying out of the self into the ultimately real. Humans are viewed as being chained to this external physical world, where we are limited in our knowledge, our joy, and our being. Final escape from this wheel of life is a total liberation from the necessity of being born into it again. The law of karma which governs our existence is a law of absolute justice—we are what we are in this existence because of the kind of life we led in a previous existence. Hence, if one is poor, it is because one *deserves* to be poor because of one's past behavior; if one is saintly, it is because one has earned sainthood and is very close to total liberation. Life's initial wants and drives for pleasure and worldly success will eventually be replaced by duty and finally by liberation to an existence of infinite knowledge, infinite joy, and infinite being. In the Hindu tradition we find various paths, known as yogas, by which each person may pursue final liberation. The appropriate yoga for each person is suited to the person's temperament and station in life: the way of work may be appropriate for one, the way of love for another, the way of knowledge for some, the way of psychological experiment for others. The ultimate goal is the same for all: union with the divine ground of all reality, the Brahman.

Buddha may be viewed as a spiritual reformer of this Hindu metaphysics. In the sixth century B.C. he breaks through the doctrine of reincarnation with the message of hope which suggests that every person may escape the wheel of life *this* time if he can understand what existence truly is for man and reach nirvana through the eightfold path which climaxes in a brilliant intuitive grasping of the infinite. Buddha's four noble truths suggest that man's condition of existence is miserable but that this misery can be overcome by magnificent spiritual effort. He tells us first that all life is suffering, or *dukkha*; second, that this suffering is caused by *tanha*, man's selfish desire; third, a message of hope that this desire can be cured; and, finally, that the way to overcome the cause of all our human suffering is to conquer our selfish drives by following his eightfold path, culminating in a total meditative absorption or "blowing out" of the self. Buddha rejects abstract metaphysical speculations, emphasizes self-effort, and crosses the caste lines that characterized traditional Hinduism. Historically we note that Buddhism flourished over the centuries in vast areas of Asia and Indochina; but in India, the land of Buddha's birth, his teachings were simply absorbed into the general Hindu culture.

Chinese Taoism, in its most philosophical version, is quite compatible with Buddhism. It stresses the underlying path or way of nature which finds man a very minuscule part of the universe. Taoism emphasizes gentleness and humility; it denounces competition and struggle. It makes much of the analogy between human existence and flowing water; the best life is the life of acceptance, of creative quietude, of flowing mildly with the currents of nature around us. The Taoist envisions the best life for man as a life which yields spontaneously to nature's way—for him, "the way to do is to be." There is no need for violence; one must lead one's life above tension. One floats with the basic life force—struggling against it will simply cause unhappiness. Humility is a crucial virtue; one must avoid aggressiveness and competition and ambition. Man does not set out to conquer nature but rather must learn to adjust himself to flow with nature. Some of the wise aphorisms from the *Tao Te Ching* expressing this view of man's role in the universe include the following: "Muddy water let stand, will clear. The ax falls first on the tallest tree."

The Taoists also taught that human values cannot be expressed in clean-cut dichotomies: opposites flow into each other and are resolved; even life and death are relative aspects of one continuum.

If we stop for a moment to assess these three views of man—the Hindu, Buddhist, and Taoist— we observe the importance placed on the inner life and the relative unimportance of the *physical* conditions of human existence. The doctrine of the moral law of karma made it easy to resign oneself to a rigid caste system and served as a rationale for a complete lack of social mobility for many centuries. We shall ask ourselves later on whether it is possible to conclude that this view of human nature could partially account for resistance to industrialization, resistance to changes in governmental and social structures, and resistance to concerns for individual rights equal to the concerns manifested in western Europe and the American continent. Is it possible that only violent revolutionary upheavals could bring about any incursions on these centuries-old cultural values? To whom and how will revolutionaries make their appeals?

May I shift now, rather abruptly, to the origins of Western views of human nature as they are found in the classical Greek period beginning as early as the sixth century B.C. In that period Greek thinkers were asking questions about the nature of the universe and proposing theories about its structure and the role of man in that structure. The first recorded scientist-philosopher theorists (men like Thales, Anaximander, Democritus, etc.) were fundamentally materialists; that is, they reasoned that all of nature (man included) derived from and was made up of one basic material substance. The search for such a substance resulted from the assumption that there had to be some unity to explain a regular and ordered universe. The actual search itself for some underlying, unifying principle for the universe was more fruitful for mankind than some of the proffered results of the search. Many would hold that science begins with the assumption that there is some basic unity to be discovered in nature. Thales purportedly held that all things are ultimately reducible to water. Democritus, along with Leucippus and others, maintained that all of reality is reducible to minute, invisible, indestructible material particles in motion called atoms. The relatively unsophisticated view of Democritus obviously was the forerunner of modern versions of atomic theory.

These early materialistic views led to some awkward implications regarding the nature and function of human beings. If man himself is through and through a material being, how shall we account for seemingly nonmaterial functions like thinking, dreaming, loving, hating, fearing, synthesizing, etc.? Can all human behavior be reduced to matter in motion? Further, since we empirically observe that material objects cease their essential being upon destruction, then we must conclude that the same thing happens when a human being dies. Death is the end of each man's existence. Yet, other thinkers wished to view man as a special creature in this universe, different in kind from other objects, and having a special kind of dignity. But can mere matter in motion be viewed as having dignity or be of infinite worth? What happens to any possible notion of permanent nonmaterial values like truth, freedom, goodness, beauty, etc., if everything including man himself is totally reducible to temporary matter in motion?

Faced with these issues, several of the pre-Socratic thinkers in the Greek world became relativists with respect to both truth and moral values. Socrates and Plato may be viewed as having reacted to this relativism and resultant demeaning of humanity. They were dominated by a search for some way of justifying rationally a belief in the dignity of the individual human personality and the permanence of human values. In pursuing this goal they provided a view of human nature which has had a profound and lasting impact on the entire Western world.

Socrates Searches for Beauty, Truth, and Goodness

Socrates viewed the search for permanent values to be so important that he dedicated his entire mature life to what he called "the examined life." He challenged all of the teachers and other men who claimed to have knowledge to critically analyze their professed truths. His claim was that even those men who seemed to possess lasting wisdom had not probed for truth deeply enough. He expressed great disdain for worldly trappings of success and stressed vigorously the need to question, to reexamine, to search for true understanding of the eternal concepts like justice and goodness. He proclaimed that "life without inquiry is not worth living for a man." This life of inquiry, the intellectual search for permanent values, was more important even than staying alive. "The wise man concerns himself far more with whether he does right or wrong than with whether he lives or dies." Socrates himself, of course, was condemned to death by a court of his Athenian peers precisely because he refused to give up his penetrating but also embarrassing and irritating cross-examinations. He inevitably showed that the claims to knowledge made by the poets, teachers, statesmen, and artists were superficial.

The Soul

In Plato's philosophical dialogue, *The Phaedo*, Plato has Socrates as the principal character present a view of human nature which stresses the importance and permanence of the rational soul. The Greek term for soul was *psyche*, which literally meant "breath" or "breath of life." Thus the soul was for both Socrates and Plato the immaterial principle of life possessed by any object which could be said to be alive. They held that man, as we find him in nature, is made up of a material body and an immaterial soul. Birth was defined as the union of a soul (life-giving principle) with a physical body. "The soul comes to the body bringing life." Death, then, would be the separation of soul and body. These views obviously were to have an important impact on Aristotle and on the doctors of the Christian church.

Socrates mused that since death is the separation of the soul from the body, the philosopher is in some sense "practicing dying all the time," for the philosopher was continually probing for truth, seeking to grasp the intellectual (nonmaterial) essences of things apart from the corrupting interference, distortions, and distractions of the body. He was attempting to grasp the concepts of beauty or goodness themselves directly, apart from the finite examples of them to be found in material objects. This emphasis on the dual nature of man (body and soul) is later to find most extreme expression in the Christian writers like St. Paul ("the spirit indeed is willing but the flesh is weak") and St. Augustine. In *The Phaedo*, Plato has Socrates presenting several arguments aimed at showing that since man's soul (his life principle) is immaterial and hence not subject to destruction or corruption like matter and since it is most like the immaterial ideas that are permanent (beauty, truth, goodness), the soul also is most likely to be permanent and therefore will continue to exist after separation from the body. In this view, a rational soul might even continue functioning (since its function is thinking) without a body. The soul of an animal or plant would require a body for its life functions of nutrition, growth, reproduction, movement, sensation, etc., but a rational soul might well continue to think without a material body.

Ideas Are Real

The crucial notion of human nature we obtain from Socrates and Plato is that the spiritual (nonmaterial) element in man, his rational soul or personality, is likely to be more permanent and hence, in a sense, more real than his finite body. This belief in the reality of the nonmaterial led to an emphasis on *ideas* rather than on things. The fundamental ideas or principles are more permanent, hence more real, than individual objects. For example, it would seem more important for an engineer to understand the permanent intellectual principles of bridge building than to know merely the temporary structure or materials of one particular finite bridge. For one who wishes to make value judgments it seems more important to understand what "goodness" is first if one is to judge this action or this person as a good or bad one. But this kind of understanding is clearly an intellectual process and indeed the process that is most unique to man as one of nature's creatures. Thus it would seem that man, as distinguished from other species, is first and foremost to be viewed as a rational being. His most distinguishing characteristic is his ability to reason.

Plato's Psychology

In Plato's *Republic* we are given a rather primitive psychological theory of man's essential nature. Plato draws an analogy between the individual man and an entire political society which is, as it were, the individual "writ large." In the ideal society, Plato discerns three basic functions and hence three types of persons who pursue these functions. Some persons must provide the basic life necessities like food, clothing, buildings, etc.; these persons may be referred to as the *workers*. Others must provide for right order in the society, implementing laws and seeing that they are obeyed and defending the society against external enemies. This second group of individuals may be called the *soldiers*. Finally, some persons must be responsible for making the laws for the society; these may be referred to as the *rulers*. The ideal society then, according to Plato, will function harmoniously when each of these three classes of people provides its function well and does not attempt to usurp the function of the other classes. In terms of virtues we must expect that the workers need to be characterized by *temperance* (they work most closely with material things and are likely to succumb most readily to physical excesses); the soldiers, by *courage* (they must remain loyal in the face of bribery and danger); and the rulers, by *wisdom* (those who legislate for all must be the wisest and morally best). When these functions are properly pursued in harmony, we then say that the society is characterized as a *just* society. Plato suggests that the virtue of justice is precisely this—the harmonious interaction of wisdom, courage, and temperance.

With the example of the ideal society in mind, Plato suggests that each individual man possesses a parallel structure in his makeup. We have the bodily *appetites* (corresponding in function to the workers), we have a *will* (corresponding in function to the soldiers) and an *intellect* or *reason* (corresponding to the rulers). In the just man, the good man, each of these functions will be carried out properly, and the proper function of reason is to rule the will and the appetites. Whenever the appetites or the will try to take over, we find inner turmoil in our lives. Thus the good life is to be found in the man whose reason is always dominating his behavior. Plato had already provided a rebuttal to Hobbes's later view of man's nature as savagely egoistic and basically amoral. Plato would have suggested to Hobbes that in the state of nature justice was indeed possible and necessary for each man, for each needed to live the properly balanced life with reason guiding his will and his appetites. In Plato's view, when a man is characterized by egoistic savagery or greediness, it is not a natural state of affairs, it is not an expression of his nature. Rather, such a state of human behavior represents an imbalance, a disharmony, indeed a total disturbance of man's "intended" nature.

Aristotle and Teleology

To speak of man's "intended" nature is to suggest that what man is supposed to become has been determined somehow in advance, to suggest that there is some sort of master plan in nature. In a sense, this was precisely Aristotle's position. Aristotle maintained that all things in nature have a specific goal, end, or purpose. The Greek word for "purpose" is *telos*, hence this view is often called teleology. Aristotle would suggest that there is a great deal of empirical data available to confirm this hypothesis about nature. When one plants an acorn, if anything comes up at all it will be an oak tree. Every time. If that acorn does achieve all that it can become, if it attains its final end or purpose, it will be a mature oak tree. It is not necessary that the acorn should develop; it could be dug up and eaten by a hog. It could rot for lack of moisture. It could grow a bit and then be knocked down or damaged. But if it realizes its total potential—it will be a mature oak tree. So, too, with all of the objects in nature; each has its specific end or purpose, its *telos*.

According to Aristotle the final end at which things aim is precisely what men call *good* for each thing. Since man is one of nature's creatures, we should expect to find that man is no exception to the teleological hypothesis; he also must have some final purpose, some highest good. In developing this view Aristotle notes that this natural goal for man must be consistent with the kind of being he is and must be related to whatever uniquely makes a man to be what he is and not something else. As a living being man shares the life functions of plants (nutrition, growth, reproduction) and animals (additionally, sensation and local motion). But man has at least one life function not shared by plants and animals: man is the animal who thinks, who reasons. Hence his special goal or purpose *as man* must be related directly to his use of reason. Aristotle was more firmly attuned to man's material existence than either Socrates or Plato. He held that while man's reasoning is an active function of the intellect (rational soul), nevertheless the process of knowing must begin with the sense perception of real material objects. "Nothing is in the mind that was not first in the senses." The Platonic view often seems to suggest that the human mind can know universal ideas directly without abstracting concepts from sense experience of individual objects.

Choice

In discussing moral action, Aristotle assumes that man can freely and rationally (hence responsibly) follow moral rules and choose voluntarily to perform actions guided by his own reason. Aristotle devotes considerable attention to the conception of man's voluntary actions for which he can be held morally responsible and involuntary or coerced actions which require a different evaluation. One of his profound observations was that we use our reason to deliberate "not about ends but about means." We may take this to mean that the "end" for man, his final goal, is not a matter of choice. We cannot choose not to be rational animals whose goal is the activity of happiness. We may choose to die or maim ourselves or refuse to develop our rational functions, but we cannot choose to become a being with some other essence than that of man. If we develop all that our nature possesses, become all that we can become, we shall be mature men, exercising rational functions in an excellent manner. Thus, all of the choices we make are restricted to the alternative actions available to us. The proper choices (those which are morally virtuous) will make us more fully developed human beings. Improper choices will demean our humanity but will not make us members of another species. Aristotle sometimes speaks of the life of contemplation (intellectual virtue) as leading to a higher kind of happiness but as being almost beyond ordinary humanity. The view of Aristotle and the classical Greek world in general will bear serious scrutiny when contrasted with that of Sartre and other contemporary existentialist thinkers who question seriously the notion of any fixed human essence.

One Swallow Does Not Make a Summer

The kind of happiness proper to man as envisioned by the Greeks mentioned here does not come in spurts or in single actions or over a short period of time. Aristotle tells us that "one swallow does not make a summer" nor does one good action make a man virtuous. Happiness is an activity to be viewed over an entire lifetime. Just as the writing of one grammatically perfect sentence does not make one a grammarian, so, too, one morally good action or one day of fruitful contemplation does not make a man good or wise. Thus, both Plato and Aristotle often advise us not to look for specific rules of behavior which will govern every instance but rather to go find the wise man, the man of excellent and constant character, and to imitate his life. Good character is not an episodic thing but rather describes the man whose integrity is consistently dependable and predictable. He is, in all things, eminently rational.

Implications

Reflecting on the view of man's nature held by Socrates, Plato, and Aristotle, we can see how influential this position has been in the Western world for many centuries. The emphasis on man's rational capacity along with its identification with the human soul have dominated most Western religious views of man and his possible destiny. It would not be an exaggeration to suggest that this view of man's essence has exerted powerful influence in the framing of constitutions, in civil and penal legislation, and in social structures. To view man as, first and foremost, a rational being, capable of moral judgment and free choice, is to view him as a being with dignity, responsible for his behavior. Such a view requires that each mature man should have a say in decision-making processes that affect him. It conflicts with the Hobbesian notion that men will accept restraints on their egoism only out of fear of an all-powerful enforcer. It makes rational behavior the ideal goal for all humans; it demands the control of the will and the appetites by reason. It places a high premium on the character training of the young and on educational experiences of the mature. It suggests that legislators ideally must be both wise and good—both intellectually and morally virtuous. Finally, it holds out for analysis a direct relationship between what man *does* and what man *is*. Knowing what man's potential is, knowing what he *can* become, determines what his moral obligations are. What man ought to *do* depends upon what man ought to *be* which is discovered by examining the essence of the species, man. For the Greek thinkers mentioned here, the central concern was very clear—man's ultimate goal, happiness, is to be experienced in the development of the best and most unique thing about his nature: his rationality.

It comes as a shock to many contemporary Christians to learn that their sophisticated notion of the human soul as a spiritual substance separable from the body does not derive wholly from the scriptures of their religions. The early fathers of the Christian church, especially St. Augustine, were very much influenced by Plato's view of the human soul. Thomas Aquinas and his scholastic followers promulgated theological positions which were also Platonic but were even more influenced by the arguments of Aristotle. Plato's idea of the good, viewed as the highest of the pure forms, becomes identified through the neoplatonists and Augustine with the Judeo-Christian notion of a personal, permanent, infinite god whose essence is perfect goodness. Christian notions of a life after death are supported by early arguments for the permanence of the rational soul, found particularly in Plato. Scholastic philosophers and theologians from the middle ages up to the present time have begun their studies with the works of Plato and Aristotle because of their extreme compatibility with the religious view of man as a rational personality housed in a material body which distracts the essential functioning of the mind and the will.

The Judeo-Christian view of man always carries with it the perspective of human nature with an ultimate purpose, a purpose given to man by a supreme personal deity who has not only placed man in the world with this purpose but has actually intervened in man's history to make that purpose known. In some periods of Western history this influence has been viewed as stagnating, with the masses of European men in the middle ages accepting the lowest conditions of existence with the promise of a better life in another world after enduring suffering in this one. In other periods of development the view of man as the highest of God's creatures and master of the other species has been credited for daring advances in science and technology which have improved man's physical existence and multiplied his educational opportunities. If man's reason is closest to the essence of God, then man may use that reason to influence his own history. The view of each individual person having infinite worth encourages conceptions of individual human rights and fosters philosophies with the most concerns for development of individual potential. History from this point of view could be interpreted as a linear and unending record of man's rational progress.

We might pause for a moment to reflect on a more pessimistic view of human nature as expressed in Thomas Hobbes's *Leviathan* in the seventeenth century. Hobbes's view is of special interest to this audience because military professionals have been viewed frequently as Hobbesian, that is, as holding similar views of man's nature. Hobbes held that in the state of nature, all men have an equal right to everything. He also held that "of the voluntary acts of every man, the object is some good to himself." Man, in this view, is the perfect egoist, selfish beyond all else. The difficulty Hobbes envisages in a world where every person has a right to everything and where every person is totally egocentered is that no one is safe—there is no guarantee of survival for anyone. Hobbes's own words provide such a graphic picture of man in this state of nature that they should be read firsthand. He says, "Hereby, it is manifest, that during the time men live without a common power to keep them all in awe, they are in that condition which is called war; and such a war, as is of every man, against every man."[1]

He continues on to claim:

> In such condition, there is no place for industry, because the fruit thereof is uncertain, and consequently no culture of the earth; no navigation, nor use of the commodities that may be imported by sea; no commodious building; no instruments of moving . . . no account of time; no arts; no letters; no society; and which is worst of all, continual fear, and danger of violent death; and the life of man, solitary, poor, nasty, brutish, and short.[2]

From this harsh, realistic view of human nature, Hobbes concludes that reason will dictate certain behavior to men who wish to survive. He provides a primitive social contract theory, suggesting that men will give up some of their unlimited rights in their own interest and enter into a contract with other men who also agree to give up their unlimited rights. For Hobbes, moral restraint only enters man's existence after an agreement is made and some common power of government is established to enforce the agreements and make laws. But man's nature does not change just because he enters into a societal compact, so Hobbes insists that the power given to government must be so strong that men will live up to their agreements out of fear of this central power. Without this fear they would soon reassert their own egoistic behavior patterns. Moral restraint is not part of man's nature but must be legislated. Since, in nature, all men have a right to everything, there can be no injustice, no immorality, no matter what actions men perform until such time as they come under the jurisdiction of a governing power, created by contract.

One can easily see that such a position on human nature would lead to the expectation of inevitable wars and would lead to the placing of the strongest possible kind of power in the hands of central government. John Locke, who also proposes a contract theory of government does not begin with such a brutal picture of the nature of man. Locke suggests that even prior to any formal societal structure, man's fundamental rights are restricted when they might infringe upon the rights of others. Locke, unlike Hobbes, insists on a natural right of private property based on the labor a man has expended on the property in appropriating it to his own use. One major reason for entering into a contract with others is to acquire security for one's own property. Thus, the powers that governments have over men would not be so strong on this view of man as on the view of Hobbes. Hobbes would reserve one fundamental human right under governmental structures, namely, the right to life. Locke would reserve a large number of individual human rights including, of course, life, but also including the right to private property as based on the labor man expends on the use of that property. Both Hobbes and Locke see man's reason as dictating their conclusions about natural human rights and the need for some sort of mutual consent in order to form protective governments. Most clearly, on Locke's view, governments derive their powers only from the consent of the governed, and he insists only the majority can have the right to legislate. When Thomas Jefferson and other American revolutionaries include their views of human nature in their political treatises, they emphasize this tradition of individual rights, personal dignity, equality of possession of human rights, etc. British thinkers like John Stuart Mill would later insist upon concern for the greatest good for the greatest number in society, but include in this insistence a vast area of individual behavior over which governments should have no control.

Shortly after the period of the American Revolution, the great German philosopher Immanuel Kant was writing his important works which led to the so-called period of romanticism in Europe. Kant makes man's reason the predominant fact about man's nature and suggests that nature must have intended some higher existence for mankind than mere well-being or survival, for instinct alone would have sufficed for that purpose. The fact that man has reason should lead him to conclude that his higher purpose involves the development of the good will, operating always with the intention of fulfilling one's moral duty. Rational man is viewed by Kant as a being of infinite worth, an end in himself, whose rules of behavior derive from his autonomous reason, which, if operating correctly, will be completely consonant with the rational rules of all other autonomous men. Thus Kant is able to announce his Categorical Imperative: "act according to that maxim which you can at the same time will to be a universal law," or alternatively, "so act as to treat humanity, whether in your own person or in that of any other as an end in itself, never as a means only." Kant sees man as both a lawgiver and a citizen of a kingdom of ends—his reason determines the laws which he himself obeys and such autonomous behavior is what Kant means by freedom of the human will.

Our time limits do not permit us to stop for a look at human nature through the eyes of those German thinkers who followed Kant, even including Fichte and Hegel, for I would like to move to a consideration of man as Karl Marx and Nietzsche and the contemporary existentialists have seen him.

The Marxist view of man would perhaps not have persisted in its present variety of interpretations had it not received the official blessing and adoption by a strong political party. Key concepts in this view of human nature to which we should pay special notice are the Marxian notion of man's self-alienation, the emphasis on materialism, the dominant role attributed to economic productiveness, the labor theory of value, and the view of private property.

Much attention has been directed recently in the Western world to the early writings of Marx, those preceding the *Communist Manifesto* and *Das Capital*, because of the view of human nature which is contained in these earlier works. Most particularly, Marx's view of man's self-alienation has received concerned interest.

Marx's view of man's alienation no doubt grew from the initial views of Hegel who saw nature as the unconscious concrete manifestation of absolute spirit which is becoming known only through man's consciousness. Man's understanding of nature is nothing more than spirit becoming conscious of itself. When man sees objects as external to himself, he sees them as alienated from the knower. Unlike Hegel, however, Marx does not place emphasis on man's spiritual being, indeed he places total emphasis on the material aspects of man's existence in nature. He takes from Feuerbach's criticism of religion the view that man's *religions* are expressions of his self-alienation. Marx sees the goal of human nature to be that of a creative, productive being improving nature by his labor on material objects but alienated both from nature and the objects he works on because of the conditions of work in the industrial societies of the nineteenth century. Because man cannot achieve fulfillment in the social, political, and economic environment in which he exists, he invents religious myths including another world in which he can find an idealized form of happiness. This dependence on an invented world keeps man from seeking meaningful happiness in his own real material world. Religion serves as his opium, lulling him into submission and acceptance of his exploitation from the capitalist classes. But it is not enough to criticize religion as Feuerbach did; thinking about injustices will not correct them. Man must set aside philosophy and act; he must change the world so that self-fulfillment becomes possible for the mass of men who make up the working class, the suppressed class.

Marx sees man fundamentally as a worker, that is, man's essence is not to be found in the life of rational contemplation but rather in economic productiveness. All social and political structures are to be evaluated from this point of view. Thus the theory of class struggle developed by Marx and Engels is based on the varying changes in the method of material production which is the central historical reality, and the process itself takes the form of a material dialectic. Unlike Hegel's historical thesis which consisted in a dialectical process of *thought*, Marx's dialectic is strictly an attempt to account for *material* reality in process. Marx's materialism is not, however, a complete rejection of the existence of human minds, it is a shift in emphasis to view material reality as dominant. A general conclusion we may draw from the writings of Marx and Engels is that they totally reject the existence of any mind or idea prior to nature—they completely reject Hegelian idealism. At best, minds come into existence from nature; when matter has reached a sufficiently complex structure, *mind* is the name we give to its emergent form.

But let us reconstruct the Marxist view of the human situation for a moment. Man is a product of the economic, social, and political forces acting upon him, and these forces historically follow a dialectical pattern which issues in a class struggle between those who control the various modes of production and those who do the producing. Those who control the modes of production also control existing governmental structures, legislation, and even the society's moral rules. In Marx's era the controlling class was perceived as the bourgeois and the workers referred to as the "proletariat." Mass man in the person of the proletariat is alienated from the state, from his work, from nature, and from himself. His true essence is to engage in creative productive labor, applying his talents to nature's material objects, but this essence is thwarted by the capitalist approach to technology and production. Man cannot find fulfillment in his work on a production line and hence is alienated from his most crucial process—work. Man is alienated from the objects he produces—they are not his nor directed for his use, and he is especially alienated from other men who appropriate the products of his labor. Marx had held that the central value in society is created by the labor which man applies to nature's objects. The laborer creates value, but the capitalist takes much of that value and pays a wage in return. If Marx's labor theory of value were correct, the amount of the wages would be irrelevant: any wage that was less than 100 percent of the value produced would be an unfair, that is, an exploitative exchange. The only way this exploitation can be avoided is to abolish the capitalist approach to human production altogether. Man's alienation from his essential function, in Marx's view, cannot be overcome until the class distinction between capitalist and worker is obliterated. Since the capitalist controls the political machinery of the state, such a change will not likely come about without a violent revolution.

At the core of these difficulties which have resulted in man's alienation from his work and hence his essential humanity, Marx sees the institution of private property. John Locke had held that private property was an inalienable human right, bestowed on each man by nature as a result of his improving the property in nature by his labor. But Marx sees private property as inextricably bound up with human egoism and all of the injustices of the capitalistic system. The worker's product is viewed as the capitalist's private property, hence as alien to the worker. But the labor which produced that object is the central expression of the laborer who is now denied his self-realization, and his alienation becomes a social class alienation at the same time. But this estrangement between social classes is not normal for man and can only be overcome, ultimately, by abolishing entirely the concept of private property and the movement to some form of communal sharing—communism. If this self-alienation can be overcome for man on the social, economic, and political level, it will also be overcome on the religious level. When all class struggles cease and private property is abolished, there will be no further self-alienation and man will find a self-fulfillment in his working existence. Elimination of his estrangement will make it unnecessary for him to seek a religious world beyond his present existence and a veritable paradise will be possible for man in his present life. Without a social class structure the moral rules generated by dominant classes will also fade away and man's life will be governed by the broadest human ethics rather than class ethics.

Please note that we have focused our attention on Marx's view of human nature and not extensively on his prophetic view of history. Events seem to have proven his historical predictions false with regard to the culmination of a bitter struggle between proletariat and capitalist; indeed the rise of many other classes in industrialized countries, surpassing the laboring class in numbers, defy any convenient molding into Marx's model of economic history. His emphasis on man's economic productiveness as the central essence of his nature may be far too narrow, but his concern for self-alienation may have provided us with profound and useful insights into human existence.

As Marx envisioned the dialectic in historical process, it was characterized by class struggle and a continuing constraint on the subordinate class of men which prevented the attainment of a truly fulfilling human life style. He anticipated one final struggle in which the proletariat would triumph once and for all: after a period of dictatorship of the proletariat and the elimination of private property, society would become completely classless, complex governmental structures would disappear, and self-alienation would cease. Writing later on in the same century, Nietzsche suggests that this view of the future presents a world in which all life activity would have disintegrated. Here are Nietzsche's own words from *Beyond Good and Evil*:

> People now rave everywhere, even under the guise of science, about coming conditions of society in which "the exploiting character" is to be absent:— that sounds to my ears as if they promised to invent a mode of life which should refrain from all organic functions. "Exploitation" does not belong to a depraved or imperfect and primitive society: it belongs to the *nature* of the living being as a primary organic function; it is a consequence of the intrinsic Will to Power, which is precisely the Will to Life—granting that as a theory this is a novelty—as a reality it is the *fundamental fact* of all history: let us be so far honest towards ourselves.[3]

Nietzsche rejects both the Greek and the Judeo-Christian views of man which emphasize man's reason and foster restraining rules of morality to hold back the strong and enshrine the weak and humble. Rather, says Nietzsche, we must recognize that man's essence is essentially his will to power; will is more central to man's development and existence even than reason. Reason's sole purpose in man is to support and assist his will in its quest for power. Nietzsche believed that human nature was itself intended to evolve into a higher state, that man is to be surpassed by the new free spirit, the *ubermensch*, or superman. This evolution will not take place in a passive, mechanical nature as envisioned by the Darwinians but only through the fostering and grasping of power by those men who are not afraid of pursuing the call to strength within them.

We have noticed that the Chinese Taoists centered their life style around their view of nature. Aristotle and the medieval Christian philosophers likewise developed views of the moral life for man centered on their view of nature and natural law. Marx also placed emphasis on nature as he interpreted nature's process in seeking moral directions for man's behavior. Nietzsche follows this pattern of examining man's role in nature as well, but his emphasis is totally on the exploitative aspects of an evolving nature influenced by the doctrine of survival of the fittest. He viewed the moral teachings of most European schools which emphasized the common good, altruism, humility, restraint upon egoism, etc., as insidious teachings which were holding back the natural evolution of those free spirits who possessed the rugged individual strength to elevate the essence of man to a new and better form of existence. Nietzsche attacks both Christian and socialist views of man because of their "hatred of egoism" and considers their position to be motivated by a desire for revenge against the strong whom they would like to blame for their own condition of weakness. Nietzsche's language is particularly dramatic on this issue when he exclaims, "the *morality of paltry people* as the measure of all things: this is the most repugnant kind of degeneracy that civilization has ever yet brought into existence." He maintains that the dominant religions of Europe have succeeded in preserving the sick and the suffering and contributed to the deterioration of European man, interfering with the role which nature intended the strong to play in human progress. Man's will to life, in his terms, could be no other than a totally unrestrained and unconditioned will to power necessitating a complete transvaluation of the so-called Christian virtues.

We may view Nietzsche as one of several forerunners of modern existentialism, a view which shares the humanism of Nietzsche and Marx but which opens wider the possibilities envisioned for man's essence. Like Nietzsche, the majority of the existentialist writers reject any static notion of species for man. Most of these thinkers maintain with Sartre that man's existence precedes his essence, that is, that first a man is born, an action over which he himself has no control, no choice, but afterwards what he is to become is totally determined by the free choices of action he makes. Man, on this view, is always engaged in the process of defining himself. If one adopts the view of atheistic existentialism particularly, then this becomes a critical and agonizing task. Without a creative God who has some design for his creatures in mind, man finds himself alone, alienated in the world without guidance, and yet he must act; he must decide, and with each decision and action he is creating humanity as it were, not only for himself but for mankind. He has the dreadful responsibility for determining the essence of man. As Sartre puts the matter, this makes man "condemned to be free" and easily leads to the depressing conceptions of anguish, forlornness, and despair which frequently characterize the writings of the existentialists and in their view, the condition of human existence.

But we must terminate this survey of these varying views of human nature and reflect on what may be learned about ourselves through such a survey. Clearly our social and political institutions have been and will continue to be affected by our conceptions of man's essence. If we hold with the Hindu or Buddhist or Taoist that man's destiny is intertwined with all of nature in a mystical way, then our life styles may well emphasize passivity and gentleness. Such a view of man does not lead to massive efforts to conquer nature and harness its resources for the sole use of men—industrialization, travel, and commerce may not seem nearly so important as prayer, contemplation, and introspection. If our philosophy of man emphasizes his egoism and his will to power, then following the views of Hobbes and Nietzsche we may well find ourselves surrounded by powerful totalitarian governmental structures. And which of these theories of human nature is correct? What is man's essence, really?

If you will forgive my temerity in venturing still another position on this issue, I find much truth about man in each of the positions discussed here and the central error in each to be a similar sort of narrow and extreme emphasis. The Eastern picture of man as essentially a spiritual substance, placing emphasis on his capacity for eventually intuiting reality in an extralogical fashion is not a false view, but it is also not a total view of man. Man's intuition and his contemplative abilities are real and capable of extraordinary development, but they do not encompass all that man is or can be. The great Christian mystics have much in common with these Eastern views, although the Western Christian mystic seeks absorption in a far more personal divinity than does the Eastern philosopher. The main thrust of the Western view of man comes from the work of Plato and Aristotle, finding a sort of synthesis in the middle ages in the Christian philosophy of Thomas Aquinas. The Greek view places major emphasis on man's reason which in the Thomistic scheme is identified with the higher part of the soul of man. Aquinas, leaning on Aristotle more heavily than Plato, gives full status to man's physical nature, as well as his mind, and stresses the psychosomatic wholeness of human existence. Stress on reason naturally leads to an emphasis on human education; stress on human dignity naturally leads to some forms of participative governments. This view of man is surely fruitful, and if it errs, it does so in not making sufficient room for the intuitive and emotional capacities of man while stressing his rationality.

When Hobbes calls our attention to man's egoism, he does us a service by describing the terrors that permeate a world where every human performs every action for his own benefit. But Hobbes's view is surely too extreme; men are capable of and do perform purely altruistic actions. We behave egoistically, certainly, but not all of us all of the time. Personal survival is a very important human value as Hobbes has noted, but it is not more important than the conditions of survival nor is external physical force the only restraint that can be effectively applied to man's egocentrism. John Locke is more nearly correct when he holds that man's moral nature can operate even in an unstructured social or political environment.

Karl Marx has done us a service in calling our attention to man's essential need to be a producer; but when he explains man and all of his relationships exclusively in terms of economic production, he demeans humanity unnecessarily. Aristotle had remarked that "all men by nature desire to know" placing great emphasis on man's intellectual curiosity, but man is far more than a knowing being. Taking a cue from Karl Marx but perhaps even more from the Greek teleological tradition and contemporary thinkers like Eric Fromm, we observe that "all men desire to accomplish"—we are purposive beings. We do seek meaningfulness in our work; we do need to find something of ourselves in our daily activities; but these activities need not be restricted to material production nor do they tell the whole story of our essence. Man is not *merely* a producer.

Nietzsche also captures our imagination and enthusiasm when he describes the importance of a "will to life." However, man's complex nature cannot with accuracy be reduced to the "will to power," nor is it clear that this drive is the central human drive. Plato would have said that it is precisely the job of man's reason to control his will to power and direct it toward rational goals.

Existentialism too has made a major contribution to our understanding of human nature by its emphasis on the individual responsibility each person has for the development of his own essence. This view counterbalances Marx's belief that human values are totally determined by the economic conditions of one's environment. Marx's view that a change in the distribution of goods and in the mode of economic production could change man's essence does not seem realistic nor does the extreme existentialist view that man's essence is entirely open-ended.

A remark of Aristotle's concerning ends and means suggests a more tenable view of human nature. Aristotle commented that "we deliberate not about ends but about means," that the central human decisions involve a choice of the means to our end which is itself fixed. We can agree with the Greeks that man's essence must be associated with his complex rational function to which we must add the critical balance of his sentient nature as well. We can agree with the existentialist that each person bears the responsibility for the kind of person that he becomes, but we would maintain that his choices do not include becoming a member of a different species. Not only did we not have a free choice about being born, but we should also note that we did not have a free choice about being born a being with rational and emotional capacities. We cannot choose to have other capacities, but we may choose the manner in which these develop or even to destroy them.

We do have a need to accomplish as Marx has noted, but that need is not restricted to mere production of material goods. It can be satisfied in the aesthetic realm in art, poetry, and music; it can be satisfied in the realm of research and reflection; it can be satisfied in the working out of our service functions in any number of occupations. Marx's attempts to save man from the consequences of alienation are not entirely unlike Christianity's attempts to save man from sin nor unlike the Buddhist plan to overcome selfish desire as the root of man's unhappiness. Each view of human nature we have examined seems to concentrate on a special aspect of man's existence to make it the central focus of an ideal life style. All agree in viewing human existence as a struggle of some sort, and all prescribe ways to handle the struggle. Hobbes tells us that only the most powerful governmental structure can hold man's ego in check and guarantee an ordered society. Marx holds out the possibility of no governmental apparatus at all once private property has disappeared and alienation is overcome. The one view is clearly too harsh, the other too unrealistic. Great tragedies have sprung from undue emphasis on one or another of the aspects of man's nature which have been highlighted here.

So far as understanding human nature is concerned, the key concept appears to be *complexity*. So far as the desired behavior which issues from that complex nature is concerned, the key concept appears to be *balance.* Man's needs are many; they are social, physical, emotional, passional, and rational, and none can be safely neglected. Technology and government alike can be judged as successful or not in terms of their abilities to provide opportunities for balanced satisfactions of each of those human needs. Eastern views of man are correct in pointing out that man's intuitive spiritual nature can lead him away from his physical suffering, but man is not merely a meditative being. The Greeks are correct in seeking a balanced lifestyle for man with reason providing the ordering principle, but man is not merely rational. The Judeo-Christian view of man's dual nature and spiritual destiny provides additional support for considering man a being with dignity and of infinite worth, but this view has sometimes been abused by the very persons who maintain it. Hobbes has recognized correctly man's easy lapse into selfish egoism, but every man is not selfish all of the time. Marx correctly recognizes man's frequent alienation from his work, his religion, and even his inner self; but not every man is alienated all of the time. Nietzsche has correctly isolated man's drive for power but failed to take seriously the disastrous consequences for mankind in the fostering of unrestrained power in the hands of his free spirits. The existentialists have rightly directed our attention to the responsibility each man bears for his own contributions to his essence through his moral decisions but failed to give proper weight to the guidance which is available in the wisdom and experience of other individuals and institutions.

We must conclude that man in his essential nature is neither savage nor saint but has the potential to become either. Attempts to reduce man to a single aspect of his existence have led frequently to personal and societal disaster. What is most clear from our survey of differing views of human nature is that adoption of one theory rather than another can have a critical impact on our treatment of ourselves and of others in our personal behavior and on the types of social and political institutions we support and develop. As you study more intensively man's institutions and the questions of war and peace, it should be extremely worthwhile to probe those institutions and issues deeply enough to discover what theory of human nature lies behind them.

Notes

1. *Leviathan*, chapter XIII.
2. *Leviathan*, chapter XIII.
3. Friedrich Nietzsche, *Beyond Good and Evil*, as excerpted in Albert, Denise, and Peterfreund, *Great Traditions in Ethics* (New York, NY: Van Nostrand Reinhold, 1969), 264-65.

Chapter 3

EGOISM, GREED, AND AMERICA'S FUTURE

Greed kills. It killed Rome and it killed Athens. It killed the czars and the East German communist party. It killed most of the French aristocracy and Patco. Greed kills people and kills nations, and will kill our way of life if you let it. — James B. Brinton, editor-in-chief of *EOS/ESD Technology*, Dec/Jan 1989-90, p. 3 (the magazine of the Electrostatic Discharge Community)

I found this reflection in an obscure technical publication this month, written by an engineering editor who is genuinely concerned about the fabric and future of American society. His litany of reasons why America is "sliding into barbarism" is worth reciting if only to set the stage for our own reflections this morning on where we are with regard to societal values and where we might be going. Brinton continues:

> Already, living standards are dropping. Infant mortality is rising. Crime and drugs are growth industries. Real incomes are falling. The quality of life is declining. Your neighbors are growing unfriendly, discourteous and worried. Government is growing impotent. Schools educate less and cost more. Bridges collapse. Libraries close. There are more holes in the road and they don't get fixed. Half of what you buy falls apart and customer service is a joke. Companies are firing older employees to avoid salary, pension, and insurance costs.

Perhaps that's enough to generate our own interest in asking how well we are doing with respect to the value system that has guided us rather consistently since our national structure was formed over 200 years ago. Let's look both externally and internally. Clearly, for some years our foreign policy has turned from a bipolar view of the world in the late forties and the fifties to a

Variations of this talk have been presented several times in the 1980s and the 1990s to a variety of military and civilian audiences.

pluralistic view of international relations. Further, that foreign policy has been characterized by a clear and continuing emphasis on human rights. We made known our strong protests when champions of human rights in other countries (men like Sakharov) were silenced by their own governments. We have even intervened militarily in places like Panama when free elections were nullified by dictators. Internally, we have pursued the doctrine of equality of opportunity in recent years with a unique vigor. We have passed strong civil rights laws; we have been greatly concerned to seek justice and fairness for minority groups, for women, for the previously disadvantaged. And yet, while we have made important strides in these areas, we notice that our people are not at peace with themselves. Now, when our advances in technology have made the physical conditions of our lives so much easier and more comfortable than ever before, we find the internal life of man in disarray: human relationships seem more difficult to sustain on an intimate level; the family structure seems aimed toward disintegration; we are concerned about examples of dishonesty in all of the professions; we can't decide when it is morally appropriate to let people die, and we find ourselves almost totally bereft of public figures to admire—we have few heroes.

As we examine one form of popular nonfiction of the last couple of decades, we may discern a trend which may have begun with a healthy concern for personal worth and individual dignity but which evolved into a celebration of the self which can only be characterized as unhealthy selfishness. I am thinking of a long list of works beginning with *I'm OK; You're OK* and ending with *Looking Out For No. 1*—books like *Passages*; *Success; Power:How to Get It*; *Up the Organization; I Ain't Much, Baby—But I'm All I've Got; Your Erroneous Zones*. Each of these books may be well intentioned and may indeed have special value, but taken as a group they spell out more concern for ego success in a materialistic or interpersonal sense than they do for the essential ethical concept of human dignity. As we turn our attention to those in public service, we may well wonder if the notion of service to the society as a whole is a mere conception to which we give lip service but not real service. Have we confused the notion of the public purpose of those on federal, state, and municipal payrolls with the notion of genuine public service? Have selfishness, careerism, concern with image, and personal gain overtaken and dominated our motives to serve the greater good of society?

The classic case of concern with image and cover-up was, of course, the Watergate affair. One of the best reflections on that episode in our national life was written by Vermont Royster in the *Wall Street Journal*[1] as the dust was settling. Royster suggested that one of the many shocks of Watergate was "the revelation of the strange sense of ethics, or rather the lack of a sense of ethics, displayed by so many lawyers." He pointed out that our former president and vice-president (Nixon and Agnew) and many others who ended up with damaged reputations were graduates of law schools. The real shock was not, however, that men trained in such a distinguished profession should do bad things, "rather it was that so many of them seemed to go astray unthinkingly. Their behavior was not that of the intentionally dishonest man, the bank robber who knows full well what he is doing. Rather it arose from a kind of moral myopia that led them to do things without seeing any moral issues at all."

The scandals, of course, have not been restricted to lawyers in public office. We have had revelations of illegal political contributions by large self-interested corporations. Scandals have touched other professionals including congressmen, doctors, judges, governors, and our intelligence and law enforcement agencies. In the teaching profession we witnessed a remarkable escalation of grades at the same time that the actual performance of students on standardized exams like college boards and graduate record exams declined measurably. Karl Menninger reported a few years ago that family studies had revealed that "the average child of ten in the United States has already developed a noncondemning attitude toward cheating." And in the military profession we have had our own ethical concerns: the My Lai affair, the issue of false reporting focused around General Lavelle, the infamous "body count" and other statistical policies which caused dishonest behavior, the recruiting scandals, the Iran-Contra affair, fraud in defense contracting, the persistence of careerism, and the insidious growing replacement of professional values with the values of the marketplace.

This state of affairs has finally gotten our attention. Professional schools have returned to the practice of offering courses in ethics; conferences on human values have become extremely popular. Ten years ago there were 35 ethics institutes in the U.S.; today there are more than 600. In the military we note that senior- and middle-level service schools in all branches are offering courses in or sponsoring symposia on professional ethics. But we should remind ourselves that ethics courses can address the problem of moral myopia; they can make us morally sensitive and capable of better reasoning about moral issues; but in themselves, they carry no guarantee of changing ethical conduct.

Let me hasten to state that I am not claiming that our society has invented or discovered evil in human actions. Corruption has been on the human scene for a very long time. But our awareness of it has changed and our moral language has changed. When was the last time you heard false reporting referred to as a lie—or lying, stealing, and murder referred to as sins? Has the rash of self-oriented literature mentioned earlier accompanied a generally adopted moral stance that one may do whatever he or she wishes so long as no one else gets hurt? How does one place any limits on sexual behavior, on students' cheating, on drug abuse, etc., if he starts from that sort of moral base? And what kind of moral example can we set for our subordinates and our children if our public behavior and pronouncements differ radically from our private actions? Senator Hart and Senator Biden and a host of television evangelists have provided ample examples of our unwillingness to accept blatant hypocrisy.

Royster suggested, and I partially agree, that we arrived at this position gradually through our fundamental concern for a basic human right—the right of privacy:

> We began in good course to remove the law's punishment for people's private conduct. But having removed the law's proscription, we have come to say what is not proscribed is to be approved, even promoted. We began by asking sympathy for the misguided thief or murderer; we end by excusing theft or murder by the misguided. . . So it goes. If it is bad to have a state religion, it is good to have no religion in the state. Because people differ on moral standards, our schools should not teach there are such things and help the young to find them.[2]

What kind of balanced approach can we substitute for the growing distortions of egoism that spring from our legitimate concern for individual dignity and personal responsibility? Let us become very practical in our considerations of values to see if there is something still to be said on the subject. Let me ask, just as an example, what kinds of work, what professions do we in our society value highly? Probably we could agree that the medical profession ranks fairly high in our scale of the prestige professions, and we ought to ask ourselves why this is so. Is it really because doctors make a great deal of money? Is it really because doctors are generally respected men in their communities? I suspect not; we have undoubtedly stated some effects that follow from practicing medicine, but surely the basic reason for the esteem bestowed upon the profession is that the doctor *as doctor* is intimately involved every day with a very important human value, namely, life itself and the quality of life. It follows as a result of our concern for this value that doctors are paid well and are highly respected. Similarly, we have high regard for the legal profession because of its essential concern for another important human value—justice, and we ought to take special note that if, along with Socrates, we value most not merely living, but "living well," then perhaps all of those professions whose essential function is to preserve and guarantee our *way of life* are at least as deserving of our respect as those concerned with preserving *life*.

This brings us directly back to the group of persons gathered here this morning and to other similar groups assembled around the country. In a very real and inescapable sense every person who finds himself or herself in the role of public service as a "leader," by his very function with other human beings, must be concerned with our way of life, with the conditions in which life is lived. She limits or extends the freedom of those she leads; he parcels out justice or injustice; she has the responsibility of interpreting what it means to treat herself and her subordinates with dignity. If in addition he or she wears a uniform, they will have to decide whether that "way of life" is worth the giving up of their own lives. I would hold as a fundamental principle that taking the oath of office "without any mental reservation" amounts to precisely that value commitment and places the military person under an unlimited liability.

Here we must pause to notice that the kind of morality of selfishness mentioned earlier won't work in any effective military organization. One of the prime values of the military profession is subordination of the self to the good of the whole—loyalty, obedience, courage, integrity, and selflessness—these are prime moral virtues that are more important for the military than for other professions. They are "nice-to-have" virtues in the employees of General Electric, or Texas Instruments; but they are not merely "nice-to-have" in the military profession—they are functional imperatives. One can be a liar and a cheat and dishonest in many other ways and still be an excellent artist, or nuclear physicist, or plumber, but as General Hackett and others have frequently reminded us, what the liar and cheat cannot be is a properly functioning soldier or sailor or airman. Without loyalty and obedience, without courage and integrity, without selflessness, we cannot carry out the military function.

The recent moves toward freedom and away from totalitarianism in Eastern Europe are reminiscent of Dostoevski's agonized struggle with freedom and moral responsibility in the "Grand Inquisitor." In that well-known chapter from his novel *The Brothers Karamazov*, Dostoevski has his principal character tell a story which brings a silent Christ back to earth during the Spanish Inquisition to confront the Jesuit cardinal who has been burning heretics by the hundreds. This Grand Inquisitor pictures himself as understanding the nature of man far better than Christ. Christ expected man to freely choose between right and wrong, to follow in his footsteps without coercion. The Grand Inquisitor insists that the vast majority of men are incapable of using such freedom well—they are too weak, vicious, worthless, and rebellious—and require to be told what to do by someone in authority who can guarantee their personal security. They must have, as he puts it, miracle, mystery, and authority. He berates Christ for refusing to seize earthly power, for not recognizing that only a few could attain salvation, for leaving men in misery. He claims it is his love for these hundreds of millions that prompted him to seize the reins of power in order that he might bring them earthly bread at the cost of their personal freedom. "They will gladly bring their freedom to me and lay it at my feet in exchange for bread and security."

Note the similarity in Hannah Arendt's comment from her book, *Totalitarianism*:

> The mass man who Himmler organized for the greatest mass crimes ever committed in history. . . was the bourgeois who in the midst of the ruins of his world worried about nothing so much as his private security, was ready to sacrifice everything—belief, honor, dignity—on the slightest provocation. Nothing proved easier to destroy than

> the privacy and private morality of people who thought of nothing but safeguarding their private lives.[3]

When our own selfishness, our own greed, our concern for only our own security overrides our basic obligation to our society as a whole, especially when that happens in those in the noblest professions, who are charged with the care of the whole society, what may happen to us? Could we find ourselves in the position of the Eastern Europeans of the past 50 years?

With this I wish to end these early morning reflections. Have we moved so far in the direction of selfishness and private security that we no longer wish to accept or are no longer capable of accepting responsibility for ourselves and our society? Have the values of the marketplace captured us so irretrievably that we can no longer find sufficient numbers of people dedicated to the good of all to tip the balance? Is the Grand Inquisitor correct when he says freedom and bread enough for all are incompatible for they shall never be able to share with each other?

Ladies and gentlemen, perhaps we can quietly resolve today that we will not let our own concern for self and our greed kill us and destroy this great nation we have sworn to serve.

Notes

1. Vermont Royster, "Thinking Things Over," *Wall Street Journal*, 17 September 1975, 24.
2. Royster, "Thinking Things Over," 24.
3. Hannah Arendt, *Totalitarianism*, Part 3 of *The Origins of Totalitarianism* (New York, NY: Harcourt, Brace, Jovanovich, Inc., 1973), 338.

Chapter 4

EGOISM AS A MORAL THEORY

I. Some Preliminary Concerns

> *"What's in it for me?"*
> *"Nice guys always finish last."*
> *"Do your own thing."*
> *"Watch out for Number One because if you don't, no one else will."*
> *"Of the voluntary acts of every man, the object is some good to himself."* (Thomas Hobbes)
> *"That officer is a careerist, not a professional; everything he does is aimed at making himself look good no matter who else may be harmed by his actions."*
> *"You only go around once in this life so get all the gusto that you can."*

The expressions listed above represent various ways of characterizing the view which philosophers refer to as *egoism*. Some of these statements purport to *describe* for us the way the world actually is; they tell us something about human nature which, if true, must have important implications for any view of moral conduct. Others of the statements listed are normative; that is, they attempt to *prescribe* behavior (e.g., "Do your own thing"). Following standard practice, we will refer to the descriptive view as *psychological egoism* and to the prescriptive view as *ethical egoism*.

Psychological egoism as a theory attempts to account for all human action in terms of a single motive—self-interest. This claim of the psychological egoist is usually a twofold claim: first, that human beings are so constituted that they *can* only act in their own interest, and this 100 percent of the time; and second, that as a matter of empirical fact, human being always *do* act in their own self-interest, even if occasionally their actions appear to be other-directed. In the second section of this chapter, we will elaborate this position by making use of two of the well-known sources of this view of human nature.

This chapter was first prepared in the early 1970s for use in our core ethics course and it has been reprinted several times in a number of publications.

Ethical egoism, as mentioned earlier, is a normative theory which prescribes as a moral rule that one *ought* always to act in one's own interest, that it is *right* to do so and it would be morally wrong to act contrary to one's self-interest. We shall be interested in the relationship between psychological and ethical egoism and ask whether it is possible to subscribe to both views at the same time. If psychological egoism is true, does ethical egoism make sense as a moral theory? If psychological egoism is false could one still, with consistency, be an ethical egoist? We will attempt to answer these and related questions in Section IV of this chapter. In Section III we will exemplify ethical egoism as it is fostered in the works of Friedrich Nietzsche and Ayn Rand.

II. Two Classical Views

In Book II of Plato's *Republic*, we find Glaucon presenting to Socrates a view of human nature which he claims is "what most people think."[1] This view is such a popular account that it deserves consideration, but it is clearly unacceptable to Glaucon. So he asks Socrates to explain why it is incorrect. This popular position is precisely what we have described as psychological egoism.

Glaucon tells Socrates that, in general, people really believe that injustice is better than justice and that anyone who could get away with it would always act in his own interest rather than from any sense of fairness toward others. It is only because people perceive that they cannot be unjust without getting worse back from others that they would ever consent to any system of laws that would constrain their egoistic behavior. Men do not behave honestly or fairly toward others willingly. It is only out of a sort of enlightened self-interest (for their own long-range benefit) that they would:

> Think it profitable to make an agreement neither to do nor to suffer injustice; from this they begin to make laws and compacts among themselves, and they name the injunction of the law lawful and just. This, they say, is the origin and nature of justice, which is something between the best, namely to do wrong and not to pay for it, and the worst, to suffer wrong and not to be able to get vengeance. . . . One who was able to do injustice, if he were truly a man, would never make an agreement with anyone neither to wrong nor to be wronged–he would be mad to do so.[2]

Glaucon is reflecting the view that the outward honesty and fairness practiced in society is really phony; by their very nature humans are always selfishly motivated. They set aside their immediate self-interest only because they understand that it can lead to immediate bad consequences, and they will outwardly follow rules of fairness toward others only because they perceive some good coming to themselves (they won't suffer unfairness done to them). But if you took two persons, one who appeared to be just and kind, the other unjust and unkind, and allowed them to behave in any manner they wished without penalty, then you would see man's true nature. They would behave the same.

> Then we should catch the just man in the act; he would go the same way as the unjust through self-seeking, the way which every creature naturally follows as a good, only the law leads him forcibly astray to honor fair dealing.[3]

To demonstrate this point further, Glaucon relates the story of Gyges, the shepherd, who finds a golden ring which has the power to make him invisible. Once he realizes he has this power to act invisibly, Gyges arranges to be sent as one of the messengers to the king. Using this power to act without fear of being caught, he seduces the queen, murders the king, and takes over the kingdom. Glaucon points out that any person would have acted in the same fashion as Gyges if he knew he could get away with it, because human nature is fundamentally egoistic.

> No one could endure to hold back from another's goods and not to touch, when it was in his power to take what he would even out of the market without fear, and to go into any house and lie with anyone he wished, and to kill or set free from prison those he might wish, and to do anything else in the world like a very god. . . . Surely one would call this a strong proof that no one is just willingly but only under compulsion.[4]

The view of man's nature which Glaucon espouses is not altogether different from the ignoble view held by Dostoevski's Grand Inquisitor. Socrates must now respond to this strong indictment of human nature contained in the popular description just discussed. The balance of Book II and indeed the entire remaining eight books of *The Republic* can be viewed as Plato's attempt to draw a picture of the human soul and human society which holds out far more noble possibilities than the psychological egoism contained in the popular view. His answer consists essentially in developing a balanced picture of the inner life of man whose motives are complex and not restricted to the single purpose of self-interest in the most immediate sense. Some interpreters of Plato hold, with some justification, that when he has Socrates describe the appetitive, willing, and reasoning functions of the human personality and points out that reason's function is to govern the other human activities, he is really approving a sort of enlightened self-interest. Reason ought to rule man's behavior because it has the best chance of providing him with an ordered inner harmony; the best life for man, the just life, involves being well-ordered and peaceful within. In any case, it is clear that Socrates and Plato repudiate psychological egoism; they hold that man is not always motivated by self-interest and need not be so motivated.

In Thomas Hobbes's *Leviathan*, we are given a graphic description of human nature as totally egoistic. It is Hobbes who describes every voluntary human action as self-interested. He arrives at this view of man by suggesting that in his primitive existence, without the artificial encumbrances of a social environment, man has been endowed by nature with a fundamental right to everything, "even to one another's body." Men use whatever power is available to them to acquire the objects of their own desires and may injure or kill others with impunity in this state of nature since "the notions of right and wrong, justice and injustice, have there no place. Where there is no common power, there is no law: where no law, no injustice."[5] Thus Hobbes views man's nature as almost savagely egoistic and primarily concerned with self-preservation. Altruistic motives would be totally unnatural for human beings and any system of moral rules would come not from nature but from some man-made societal institution.

This view of man's nature is so vividly characterized by Hobbes that the flavor of his own language is worth our attention:

> Hereby it is manifest, that during the time men live without a common power to keep them all in awe, they are in that condition which is called war; and such a war, as is of every man, against every man. For WAR, consisteth not in battle only, or the act of fighting; but in a tract of time, wherein the will to contend by battle is sufficiently known.[6]

Hobbes's account of man's nature leaves no possibility of its perfectibility, and only some hope of controlling individuals by force and fear of force. His description of a world in which there is no social structure to restrain man's savage propensities follows:

> Whatsoever therefore is consequent to a time of war, where every man is enemy to every man, the same is consequent to the time wherein men live without other security, than what their own strength, and their own invention shall furnish them withal. In such condition, there is no place for industry, because the fruit thereof is uncertain, and consequently no culture of the earth; no navigation, nor use of the commodities that may be imported by sea; no commodious building; no instruments of moving, and removing, such things as require much force; no knowledge of the face of the earth; no account of time; no arts; no letters; no society; and, which

> is worst of all, continual fear, and danger of violent death; and the life of man, solitary, poor, nasty, brutish, and short.[7]

Fortunately, Hobbes notes, nature has supplied man with reason which leads him to discover a number of "laws of nature" which will assist him in his egoistic task of self-preservation. Reason shows him that he cannot long survive on his own so he must agree to give up his right to everything provided that other men will agree to do the same, and enter into a social contract which will establish a common power and a set of binding laws. Agreements by themselves will not change man's egoistic nature, so sufficient power must be granted to the governmental authority to coerce men into fulfilling their agreements out of fear of common power. It is clear that Hobbes is reemphasizing the position described by Glaucon: men will not willingly act in accordance with rules of justice, honesty, and fairness, but will do so only to insure their own individual interests and security. While Hobbes offers no modern set of empirical data to "prove" that his view of man's nature is correct, he does point out that even in well-ordered societies, people act as though his estimation of man is true. Most people lock their doors, their safes, keep their valuables in vaults, go armed when they travel, etc., even when there are policemen and soldiers around to protect them. What would Hobbes say about the widespread savage looting that took place during the Los Angeles riots several years ago?

III. Selfishness Is a Virtue

We indicated at the outset that psychological egoism is not a moral theory at all but an attempt to describe how human beings as a matter of fact really do behave. Ethical egoism, on the other hand, is a moral theory which holds that men ought to behave in their own self-interest. There are many versions of ethical egoism but to typify the position we have elected to discuss two of the most widely read and persuasive of the egoist writers, Friedrich Nietzsche and Ayn Rand.

Nietzsche's view of man's nature places total emphasis on the development of the individual, indeed on the evolving of certain great spirits into "new" men, supermen who should be the next stage in the evolutionary scheme. He sees this development being held back by the traditional moral systems which he refers to as "slave moralities." In particular, Nietzsche vilifies the Judeo-Christian morality and all others that make altruism a moral virtue because these positions conceal the true nature of human existence, effectively harnessing and limiting man's fundamental will to power. Altruism, however, is a subtle expression of the egoism of the weak who seek to hold back the strong and powerful.

> The *hatred of egoism*, whether it be one's own (as in the case of the Christian), or another's (as in the case of the Socialists), thus appears as a valuation reached under the predominance of revenge; and also as an act of prudence on the part of the suffering, in the form of an increase in their feelings of cooperation and unity. . . . The discharge of resentment which takes place in the act of judging, rejecting, and punishing egoism (one's own or that of others) is still a self-preservative measure on the part of the bungled and the botched. In short: the cult of altruism is merely a particular form of egoism, which regularly appears under certain definite physiological circumstances.[8]

Nietzsche's appeal is to a new moral view of the individual which recognizes his freedom to choose in his own interest, which is to foster the essential nature of man. Competition and exploitation, even cruelty, are the proper moral qualities of the free spirit; altruism, humility, benevolence, etc., are life-ending characteristics of weakness which frustrate the natural development of the strong and powerful.

> People now rave everywhere, even under the guise of science, about coming conditions of society in which "the exploiting character" is to be absent:—that sounds to my ears as if they promised to invent a mode of life which should refrain from all organic functions. "Exploitation" does not belong to a depraved or imperfect and primitive society: it belongs to the *nature* of the living being as a primary organic function: it is a consequence of the intrinsic Will to Power, which is precisely the Will to Life.[9]

Clearly, Nietzsche's view of morality is one which makes a virtue out of selfishness; one ought to pursue his own will to power; one ought always to act in his own interest, ignoring the interests of the common herd who do not fully grasp the essence of humanity or who in resentment of the developing strong individuals attempt to limit the power of the individual. In Nietzsche's language, altruism can only foster the degeneracy of human civilization by eeping alive and praising the weak and humble which nature itself abhors. He ges a war against "the morality of paltry people as the measure of all things." seeks a transvaluation of values which will foster as good the interest of the individual who pursues rightfully his will to power, and final condem-n of altruistic ethics as the despicable doctrine of weak and paltry people.
ietzsche had thought that even the great classical philosophers had made us mistake in emphasizing man's reason as the dominant center of his

being and source of his moral precepts. He saw reason as properly suited only to assist the human will, more precisely the will to power which for him constituted the central essence of man's existence. In the works of Ayn Rand we find a contemporary analogue of Nietzsche's insistence on the primacy of special individuals and the clear moral injunction to act always in one's own interest. Rand, however, does not accept the central role of the will which characterized Nietzsche's view but rather stresses that selfishness is a *rational* virtue, demanded by objective reason. This theme permeates her well-known novels (*The Fountainhead* and *Atlas Shrugged*), and is most specifically promulgated in a small collection of her essays entitled, *The Virtue of Selfishness, A New Concept of Egoism*.

Rand attempts to accomplish essentially two tasks in promoting an egoistic ethic: first, she wishes to demonstrate conclusively that altruistic ethics is the cause of the greatest injustice and the source of totally false moral judgments; second, that rational selfishness provides the only objective set of moral standards which supports man's survival as man.

In attacking altruism, Rand pushes it to its most extreme version by stating that "Altruism declares that any action taken for the benefit of others is good, and any action taken for one's own benefit is evil."[10] She reduces altruism to the view that anything at all is right so long as it is done for the benefit of "anybody other than oneself." Thus many modern evils are laid at the doorstep of an altruistic ethics which permits great harm to, and self-sacrifice on the part of, individuals in the name of benefiting "the people." Morality in this context seems not to be the proper guide and helpmate of the individual person but almost appears to be his enemy since "he has nothing to gain from it, he can only lose." The great harm that altruism does is that it labels man's natural efforts to live as evil.

> Since nature does not provide man with an automatic form of survival, since he has to support his life by his own effort, the doctrine that concern with one's own interests is evil means that man's desire to live is evil—that man's life as such is evil. No doctrine could be more evil than that.[11]

The key to human dignity and self-respect cannot be found in pursuing altruistic ethics, therefore, but only in a life-approving self-supporting moral doctrine. Rand calls her version of egoism "Objectivism." Objectivism does not view man's life as merely that of a self-sacrificing animal but rather dignifies man's existence by more accurately defining man's values and his reason for being. She insists that "*concern with his own interests* is the essence of a moral existence, and that *man must be the beneficiary of his own moral actions*."[12] To act in one's own interests is not equivalent to doing as one pleases, however. Rand holds that there is an ultimate ground of all value that preserves morality from mere whims, wishes, or desires. That ground which serves as the only end in itself is *life*; "the concept of 'Life' . . . makes the concept of 'Value' possible." But man's life, unlike that of other living beings, is not automatically provided for; he "has no automatic code of survival . . . no automatic course of action, no automatic set of values." He is provided with *reason*, and it is through the use of this faculty that man can determine which values are crucial to his survival. His ethical rules are not whims of society nor even beliefs derived from religious orientation, but rather they are objective, rational, and necessary conditions of man's survival:

> The standard by which one judges what is good or evil—is *man's life*, or: that which is required for man's survival *qua* man. Since reason is man's basic means of survival, that which is proper to the life of a rational being is the good; that which negates, opposes or destroys it is the evil.[13]

Thus, for this form of egoistic ethics, rationality is a fundamental virtue, interpreted as making one's own decision, selecting one's own type of productive human work, never sacrificing the products of one's own mind to the opinions of others (independence and integrity). Other virtues which Rand insists must come from this view of man's moral life include honesty (don't fake reality), productiveness (self-generated), and pride (in a self-made soul). Her view of the working out of such an ethics of egoism requires a society that is itself free and productive and not governed by a doctrine (her interpretation of both hedonism and altruism) which maintains "that the happiness of one man necessitates the injury of another."

We will summarize this view of ethical egoism by citing at length from Ayn Rand's writing in order to provide the full thrust of her vigorous tying of self-interest to the moral life.

> The basic Social principle of the Objectivist ethics is that just as life is an end in itself, so every living being is an end in himself, not the means to the ends or the welfare of others—and, therefore, that man must live for his own sake, neither sacrificing himself to others nor sacrificing others to himself. To live for his own sake means that *the achievement of his own happiness is man's highest purpose*. . . . The objectivist ethics proudly advocates and upholds *rational* selfishness—which means: the values required for man's survival *qua* man. . . .
>
> The objectivist ethics holds that *human* good does not require human sacrifices and cannot be achieved by the sacrifice of anyone to anyone. It holds that the *rational* interests of men do not clash—that there is no conflict of interests among men who do not desire the

> unearned, who do not make sacrifices nor accept them, who deal with one another as *traders*, giving value for value.[14]

IV. Commentary

At the outset it is relevant to notice what may be quite obvious: The view one takes of human nature makes a significant difference in the way one treats others persons and oneself. A convinced psychological egoist may well be an authoritarian parent, a "rule book" military disciplinarian, or an advocate of maximum government power and regulation. One's estimate of human nature is also crucial to the attitude adopted toward the moral life. Glaucon's dramatization of psychological egoism through the story of Gyges' ring suggests that concepts of justice, fairness, honesty, and benevolence must always be a sham; moral virtues of this sort would clearly be phony and exhibited only under external compulsion or for the sake of developing a false reputation.

Notwithstanding these possible consequences of adopting the view that men can and do only act from self-interested motives, the question remains, is this Hobbesian view correct? Incidentally, it is worth noting that Hobbes's position is often held to entail that war among men is inevitable and that professional military leaders must generally subscribe to a Hobbesian view of human nature. But are human motives reducible to this one? Are even acts of heroic self-sacrifice really to be interpreted as self-interested? It does not appear that all the inner springs of human motivation are subject to any sort of direct inspection. The convinced psychological egoist, when faced with empirical evidence which suggests that someone has acted in a non–self-interested fashion, will insist on his theory in spite of the only factual data available. He will often say that the benevolent or altruistic action *must* have been egoistically motivated in spite of the evidence. This, of course, changes the status of psychological egoism from being a description of the way human beings behave to a largely irrefutable *a priori* thesis about how they must behave. But experience, both introspective and observational, favors the view that human motivations are complex and not simply reducible to any single tendency. Persons sometimes seem egoistically motivated, sometimes motivated by benevolence toward the welfare of others, and sometimes motivated in ways impossible to evaluate.

Suppose we assume that psychological egoism is correct, i.e., that a person can act *only* from self-interest. Does ethical egoism as a moral theory follow from this supposition? Clearly, it does not; indeed, it seems quite plausible that no ethical theory can possibly be derived from the thesis of psychological egoism. Any moral theory must be prescriptive, i.e., it must tell us how we *ought* to behave. But it makes little sense to set out a rule of behavior if we *can* only act in specific ways no matter what rules we may accept. The classical way of expressing this thought is that *"ought" implies "can."* If I *ought* to do a given action then it must be the case that I am *able* to do it and further that it is in my power to avoid doing it. It makes no sense to tell me that I *ought* to fly without wings (because I cannot). Similarly, it makes no sense to give me moral credit for doing something which I could not have avoided. These considerations suggest that if psychological egoism is true, then ethical egoism either is impossible as a moral theory or is at best superfluous.

One can perhaps make a slight concession to the possibility of ethical egoism if psychological egoism is correct. If it is true that each person can only and does pursue his own interest, it may yet be the case that some are better at self-interested actions than others and hence ethical egoism might consist in a set of rules for facilitating the pursuit of one's own welfare.

Suppose, however, that psychological egoism is false. Then, it seems clear that ethical egoism is a *possible* moral theory and the question becomes, is it a *good* moral theory? If we are to accept the views of Nietzsche and Rand, ethical egoism is the *only* moral theory that will guarantee the continued progress of man toward some higher stage of being and indeed holds out the only possibility for man's continued survival. Hobbes and Rand are in obvious disagreement on the outcome of every person's pursuing his or her own self-interested goals. Rand holds that acts of rational selfishness never will be in conflict with each other; Hobbes believed that self-interested action could lead to total chaos unless a powerful Leviathan completely controlled and limited man's egoistic nature. Hobbes held that reason would dictate severe limitations on man's egoistic actions; Rand maintains that unfettered egoistic behavior would clearly be the rule of reason. Hobbes held that man's egoism must be controlled in order for mankind to survive; both Nietzsche and Rand see the control of egoism as debilitating for the species man.

Surely, any ethical theory ought to satisfy certain criteria if it is to be judged as a good theory, and adequate, or a theory that is better than others. We are driven to consider again the nature of human existence if we are to begin any set of standards for judging egoism or any other moral theory. If the purpose of my existence is totally centered around my own personal survival and my own personal development, then ethical egoism may seem initially the moral theory to guarantee the fulfillment of my purpose. But wisdom and experience both suggest that human beings do not achieve even survival on their own—man is indeed a social being and unavoidably involved with other persons even for mere survival. Given this condition of existence, it would seem that any satisfactory moral system must account not only for individual personal development but also for one's complex relationships with other human beings.

Individual interests do in fact often conflict. Ethical egoism holds little promise for exhibiting moral ways of resolving these conflicts other than resort to force—but survival of the fittest does not itself appear to be a moral principle.

Finally, man seems to have within himself a drive toward accomplishment, a need to find some meaningfulness in his life beyond the mere living of it for himself, beyond survival. Humans want to make the conditions of humanity better—and not only for themselves. Parents want their children and their grandchildren to have meaningful, value-laden lives. From this perspective, ethical egoism seems far too narrow to satisfy human yearning. While contributing to the welfare of others may well bring a sense of personal satisfaction, the performance of altruistic actions involves something more than an indirect sort of self-interest. Promise-keeping, truth-telling, avoidance of theft, respect for the dignity of other persons—all of these types of moral behavior may well be viewed as being consistent with self-interest, but it seems clear that their moral rightness is not derived from their relationship to self-interest. Ethical egoism, by itself, involves an impoverished view of man's possible purpose; we must look elsewhere for a better balanced, more complete moral point of view.

Notes

1. The references to Plato's *Republic* are based upon the W.H.D. Rouse translation and are contained in pages 155-163 of *Great Dialogues of Plato*, (New York: The New American Library [Mentor], 1956). The references to Thomas Hobbes's position are essentially from chapter XIII of his *Leviathan*.

2. *Great Dialogues*, 156.

3. *Great Dialogues*, 157.

4. *Great Dialogues*, 157.

5. *Leviathan*, ch. XIII.

6. *Leviathan*, ch. XIII.

7. *Leviathan*, ch. XIII.

8. Friedrich Nietzsche, *The Will to Power*, as excerpted in Albert, Denise, and Peterfreund, *Great Traditions in Ethics* (New York: Van Nostrand Reinhold, 1969), 263.

9. *Great Traditions*, 264-265, from *Beyond Good and Evil*.

10. Ayn Rand, *The Virtue of Selfishness* (New York: New American Library, 1964), viii.

11. *The Virtue of Selfishness*, ix.

12. *The Virtue of Selfishness*, ix.

13. *The Virtue of Selfishness*, 23.

14. *The Virtue of Selfishness*, 27-31.

Part III

ETHICS AND THE MILITARY PROFESSION

Chapter 5

THE VOCATION OF ARMS

One of the most searing unresolved issues in the conduct of the Cold War is not the advantage of missiles over manned bombers, not which is the "best" TFX, not the use of nuclear vs. conventional weapons. It is the more serious question of people, without whom all weapon systems are as ineffective as a challenge to a fistfight by an armless man. It is the problem of how to keep servicemen in the service.

Solutions have, of course, been offered, criticisms have been leveled, alarms have been sounded. Clarence Randall, Chairman of the President's Pay Advisory Group, has endorsed a 14 percent pay increase for the military, and he favors a retirement system that would replace the present twenty-year plan. Both proposals, the administration hopes, will keep people in the service of their country longer.

Daniel Bell, in a recent article in *The Columbia University Forum*, has called the uniformed services "the military dispossessed." Because, he says, "of its outmoded curriculum, its recruitment and promotion patterns, the vested interests of the different services, and the concentration at the top levels of officers trained in older notions of strategy, [it] is ill-equipped to grasp modern conceptions of politics, or to use tools—computer simulation, linear programming, gaming theory—of strategic planning."

Morris Janowitz, in his definitive study, *The Professional Soldier*, indicates that 20 to 25 percent of the graduates of the military and naval academies (it's 50 percent among ROTC graduates) are resigning their commissions after four or five years of service. He predicts an even higher attrition among Air Force Academy graduates, because they possess skills that are more directly transferable to civilian occupations. Speaking of the ever-narrowing gap between the military and the civilian, in which the military is becoming more civilianized and the civilian militarized, Janowitz clearly sees, nevertheless, the essential role of the armed forces: "the military establishment has a special environment because it alone has the organizational responsibility for preparing and managing war and combat."

This was my first published paper on the military profession. It was coauthored by the late Paul Briand and published in *Air Force and Space Digest*, 46 (July 1963), 40-47. Reprinted with permission.

David Boroff, in his recent series of articles on the three service academies (*Harper's*, December 1962, and January and February 1963) is fearful of the very word *mission*. The mission, we assert, simply and positively establishes the threefold need of soldier-scholar-athlete for duty-honor-country. Boroff wants civilian solutions for service problems. In his article about Annapolis, for example, he makes the civilian mistake of lumping prestige and pay together, as if the two were inseparable in the American way of life: "Military service must be dramatically upgraded both in terms of prestige and pay. It should have serious importance of the kind that service in the State Department or in a high government agency currently enjoys."

The armed services themselves are not without guilt, particularly in their recruiting advertisements, when they too often beckon with material lures, too often stress pay and promotion, retirement at a young age, education and travel, in order to attract and keep young men in service for lifetime careers. The services should not, therefore, be puzzled if these same young men leave military careers for more of the same benefits in civilian life.

The U.S. government itself, however unwittingly, encourages the quick departure of the young and the bright from the services, by offering and paying out of its own pocket sometimes even greater financial rewards—by simply tearing Uncle Sam from its recruiting posters and replacing him with a defense contractor or a civil servant. The same government which trains and educates the young people it wants to keep for lifetime service often lures them into civilian jobs with higher pay—and still continues to pay the bill.

The story is bruited about almost daily in military circles how, for example, a master sergeant has not reenlisted but has taken a high-paying job with quicker promotion prospects, in an electronic firm—a defense subcontractor; or how a colonel has resigned his commission (just a few years before retirement), to become a vice president of an aircraft corporation—a defense contractor; or how a young Academy or ROTC graduate has left the service to become a civil servant at a five-figure salary.

These people who do resign argue that they are, after all, still working for the government, either directly or indirectly; it is still the same old Uncle Sam who is paying their wages. No one challenges this argument. The challenge—and there is one—is, bitterly and realistically, in quite another place. It cannot be seen on posters, or found in the offers of promotion and pay and retirement, in or out of the service. The challenge is to, and in, the minds and hearts of all Americans.

The serious soul-searching of many men as they decide whether to stay in or leave the service is often testimony to their understanding of the importance of the problem. But all too frequently the reasons they give for leaving, and indeed for staying in, are almost irrelevant to the central issues. They confuse the real reasons with their given reasons.

There is the easy confusion about "work"; it is a job, just another way of making a living. If it is for them a job, then we ask: Is it something for which they strive to be paid more and more for doing less and less so that they might have more time in which to do nothing? Is it what they do during their waking hours? What if it is disliked, boring, yields no sense of fulfillment or satisfaction? And suppose this happens every day, in or out of the military?

One of the most vital human needs is fulfillment in work. Aristotle knowingly observed that all men by nature desire to know—we are curious beings; but all men by nature also desire to accomplish—*we are purposive beings.*

Every man, every military man, needs to feel satisfaction in some accomplished task. The life in which this need is never or seldom realized is robbed of something essentially human. The serviceman's legendary gripe, or the anxious, bewildered cry of loss from our "beats" and angry young men (our stay-at-home, lost generation), is more like an agonized wail at not having found themselves in any activity. They have not made, or care not to make, the necessary distinction between a job and a profession, or between a profession and a vocation. For each, in ascending order, gives a greater sense of involvement, fulfillment, and satisfaction.

If a job is something to get paid for doing from eight to five, if it is something to leave behind on the way home, then it becomes something distinct and separate from our total lives. If it is a profession, then it surrenders to a larger part of our lives; there is a greater involvement, a more total commitment. We see this heartening sense of accomplishment in many doctors, some lawyers, and a few great teachers.

When a man's work is his vocation, however, then we see a total engagement of his life and personality, a complete outlet for self-expression, a conclusive realization of his potential. Such a vocation clearly marks and distinguishes the best of what a good man has in him. Moreover, any work may be a vocation for any man, if the degree of his involvement and the quality of his skill and dedication are of the highest order. John W. Gardner, President of the Carnegie Corporation of New York, has acutely perceived this important distinction: "The society which scorns excellence in plumbing because plumbing is a humble activity, and tolerates shoddiness in philosophy because philosophy is an exalted activity, will have neither good plumbing nor good philosophy. Neither its pipes nor its theories will hold water."

The Gardner comment, unfortunately, all too often holds true in America. We are annoyed by the repaired automobile, washing machine, stove, or refrigerator that still does not work because the mechanic was not *really* a mechanic; the children's shoes that break down after thirty days because the cobbler was not really a cobbler; the house that cracks along the walls and ceilings because the builder was not really a builder. Can a nation last when things are not made to last? Not unless everyone from the philosopher to the plumber, from the general to the private, can look upon his work as a vocation. Otherwise, each falls far short of what his own life and talents can offer society. Society falls short to the degree that each man, successively, fails in living the life of a total human being.

Moreover, a philosopher or a plumber or a soldier must be able to live with himself before he can live with others; he must be true to his own talents, interests, and capabilities before he can genuinely contribute to life around him. That sailor or airman who remains in a job merely because of financial security, while his abilities lie elsewhere in civilian life, is untrue to himself and to his country. Although there may be family and economic pressures that make it practically impossible for him to pursue his "vocation," these considerations do not alter the fundamental principle. While it is flagrantly obvious that human nature is not perfect, it is still true that if men fail to seek its ideal conditions, then there is little hope left for growth and progress.

The military life can be a perfect vocation, although the short-termer may look at it merely as a job and the career officer and airman may regard it primarily as a profession. No one questions the necessity of military service in wartime, and all question the man who fails to answer his country's call. But what of military service in time of peace? The serviceman is then viewed, even by veterans, with distrust. He is taunted as an economic leech, draining off the lifeblood of the nation—$56 billion for fiscal year 1964, about half of the national budget! Sensational best-selling novels, like *Fail-Safe* and *Seven Days in May*, portray him (to his incredulous astonishment) as one blindly willing to destroy almost half of the entire world or even as an exponent of treason. He is even accused, by Fred J. Cook in the book *The Warfare State*, of being part of a sinister military-industrial combine hopeful of taking over the country. Incredibly, he bears these libels in bristling but mute indignation. The prestige and respect that the man in uniform enjoyed in wartime is just as clearly lost to him in periods of peace. He is suspect. He is tolerated.

These ironies encase a hard paradox in our civilization: The man who preserves life, like the medical doctor, enjoys the highest prestige (we are "scared to death" to die and we will pay almost any price to live); yet the soldier or sailor or airman, in a hot or cold or lukewarm war, who is prepared to die, if need be, in the defense of his country, who is sworn to preserve the very conditions that make life possible for others, enjoys no such prestige.

The man who voluntarily puts on the blue or green uniform of the service implicitly, if not explicitly, commits himself to the principal view that there are some values in life worth more than life itself. There is something worth the risk of life. That something is the way life is lived. All servicemen discover themselves the allies of Socrates, who lived and died with the unshakeable conviction that a decent man cherishes far more whether he does right or wrong (his way of life) than whether he lives or dies.

Is it maudlin in our time for a young American to say to himself, as others have before him: "I regret that I have but one life to give to my country" or to say: "Is life so dear or peace so sweet as to be purchased at the price of chains and slavery? Forbid it, Almighty God!"? Is it soft to mean it when you say: "Better dead than red!"? Thankfully, there are still thousands of Americans in uniform, who despite temptations to life in mufti; who in spite of the criticisms of pedagogues about their training and education, of economists about their high spending, of technologists about push-button missiles that will replace them; who when the order is given to proceed to Vietnam or Cuba hold to a simple unspoken belief: Death, if necessary, so that others may live.

Certainly the prestige accorded a doctor is deserved because the doctor's essential function is aimed at an important value: the preservation of life. But the essential function of the armed forces of a free nation is aimed at an even higher value: the preservation of the very conditions that make life possible. We propose that the military profession has the right to the respect given to other professions. And from the point of view of its essential function, it is perhaps an even more "noble" profession than most others.

But more than a job, and more than a profession, military life can be a completely satisfactory vocation. Military service in the United States today ranges over a number of specialized activities. An ensign may be an expert in nuclear physics, or a sailor a deep-sea diver; a captain may be a jet pilot, or a soldier a paramedic; a lieutenant commander may program computers, or a chief petty officer command a tug; a major may be a neurosurgeon, lawyer, political-science professor, or rabbi—or an airman a cryptanalyst. And the astronauts, their wearing of civilian clothes notwithstanding, are *Lieutenant Colonel* John Glenn, *Lieutenant Commander* Scott Carpenter, *Major* Virgil I. Grissom, *Commander* Alan B. Shepard, Jr., *Major* L.Gordon Cooper, and *Commander* Walter Schirra—all officers in the uniformed services of their country.

Thus a serviceman's specialty may by itself take on the distinction of a vocation. But if, for example, the Air Force pilot has found his vocation in flying, what difference does it make if he should resign and fly for a civilian airline? The difference, to us, is crucially important. Military life adds significance to the vocation of the captain-pilot which the airline pilot need never ponder. The military vocation, whether of pilot, deep-sea diver, or cryptanalyst, requires a further dedication, an extra sense of responsibility. Unlike the civilian doctor, lawyer, or teacher, who practices his essential function all the time, the military man sometimes seems so far removed from his that it is difficult for him to keep his primary purpose in mind. Regardless of these hazards, however, this full commitment to a higher cause by a serviceman guarantees the preservation of a way of life which permits any man to seek his own work anywhere. It is a vocation that allows others the right to pursue their own vocations.

Despite the call to higher values in a military career, there are admittedly many personal restrictions which seem to prevent the free expression of a total personality in the service—an indispensable requirement before work can become a vocation. Zealous critics will say that anyone who has ever served "knows" that military men take orders; that the "military mind" is stagnant, conservative, and unoriginal; that many assignments force a man into a job he hates, to work for a superior he dislikes, and in a climate he abhors. And they ask, How can these conditions make a vocation out of work?

We say that in the large these are glib critiques that do not square with the facts of present-day military life. We do not deny the existence of rigidity in the military. We suggest rather that where it occurs it is of the same brand that afflicts any large organized segment of our society.

But if there is a "military mind" in the service today, it belongs not to the American counterpart of Colonel Blimp, but to what Morris Janowitz, with keen insight, calls "the intellectual officer" or "the military intellectual." Janowitz describes the intellectual officer as the soldier (his inclusive term for all servicemen) "who brings an intellectual dimension to his job. His intellectual quality is held in check by the needs of the profession. He sees himself primarily as a soldier, and his intellectuality is part of his belief that he is a whole man."

"The military intellectual," on the other hand, "is a markedly different type. Although he is a professional soldier, his attachments and identifications are primarily with intellectuals and intellectual activities. He would have no trouble shifting from military to university life, for his orientations are essentially scholarly. He is generally denied, or unequipped, for the highest command posts, as would be the case with intellectuals in civilian society. His position is essentially advisory, but, in the military setting, the advisory post is institutionalized and accepted," Janowitz writes.

These uniformed intellectuals, with or without Ph.D.'s, are in the ranks, but there is a great need in the military life not only for these thinkers, but also for thinkers from all disciplines—military, scientific, and humanistic. The political, scientific, economic, social, and cultural implications of policy-level, military decisions made today must be studied and evaluated by the most knowledgeable minds in the nation, minds that must also belong to men in uniform. And this creative and analytical thinking must be joined to the most responsible kind of self-discipline in the taking and giving of orders. In the military man, the two must work inextricably together, for discipline and creative thinking are not mutually exclusive. Indeed, they are mutually dependent.

If the military wishes to ensure for itself the dignity and prestige which it rightly deserves because of its very purpose for being, then it must assume certain responsibilities. It must squarely face the issue of vocations as any thinking human being must in any type of work. It must be convinced that the values at stake are worth a total commitment. If it wishes to merit the respect of others, it must first respect itself; and internal respect for the military way of life begins when all servicemen view it not as a job, not as a profession, but as a vocation.

This same attitude must then extend and pervade the thinking of all Americans—of the parents of young men considering the service as a career, of the businessmen alarmed at the military use of tax dollars, of professional men unaware that there are others as dedicated as they, and finally, of the lobby groups who pressure some congressmen into favoring the represented nonuniformed government services over the nonrepresented uniformed services of that same government.

If the American way of life is really more important than life itself, then the military life is, indeed, a noble calling. The vocation of arms deserves the total dedication of thoughtful men and the respect of free men everywhere.

Chapter 6
THE AMERICAN MILITARY: THEIRS TO REASON WHY

In his often-quoted poem "The Charge of the Light Brigade," Alfred Lord Tennyson characterized an attitude toward military men that smolders perennially but glows brightly during periods of national frustration.

> Theirs not to make reply,
> Theirs not to reason why,
> Theirs but to do and die.

We are concerned, all of us, about a picture of a profession that leaves us feeling that a man must give up his rationality, his very creativeness, the source of his dignity as a man, in order to play his role as a soldier. Tennyson's dramatic portrayal conjoins the soldier's unquestioning obedience with the qualities of courage, loyalty, and determination but leaves us with the inference that not all military leaders are as bright as they should be, even in things military: "Someone had blundered."

History records many blunders, costly in human lives, made by military leaders who were just not quite equal to a battle or a war or a world that did not follow yesterday's pattern. General Sir John Winthrop Hackett in his 1962 Lees Knowles Lectures, published as *The Profession of Arms*, cites the devastating British defeat at the Battle of Loos in World War I as a prime example of faulty, unimaginative, and inflexible military leadership. The British advanced twelve battalions against entrenched German machine gunners and lost 8,000 of 10,000 men, while the German losses were "nil." Of this tragedy, Sir John said:

> these generals were not all wicked men nor always stupid men and they were very rarely cowards themselves. Their errors were more those of blindness than malignity. Where they failed was in understanding the techniques of their time. . . . Whatever their many good qualities, they were often unequal to their task, and

This chapter was first published in *Air Force Magazine* in February, 1971. Reprinted with permission. Many variations of these ideas were presented in the 60s, 70s, and 80s under the title "The Military Mind."

> when they made mistakes the results were often appalling, with the most serious consequences for western society.

History further discloses certain practices in the military organizations of various countries which deemphasized positive military achievements and perpetuated negative attitudes toward the profession. Promotion by purchase, class discrimination between soldier and officer, and bestowing commissions upon the aristocracy all did little to relate intellect and leadership ability to military advancement. These practices, along with such errors as that committed by the British generals at the Battle of Loos, may have prompted H. G. Wells' comment in his *Outline of History* (1920):

> The professional military mind is by necessity an inferior and unimaginative mind; no man of high intellectual quality would willingly imprison his gifts in such a calling.

Popular literary lampoonings of military leaders (see how high-ranking officers are characterized in *Seven Days in May*, *From Here to Eternity*, *Fail Safe*, *Dr. Strangelove*) or dire warnings against the military-industrial complex (Fred Cook's *The Warfare State*, John Kenneth Galbraith's *How to Control the Military*) help us to understand current attitudes toward "military minds." If we add an extremely unpopular war in Vietnam which, though not initiated by our military leaders, must be waged by them, the *Pueblo* incident, the My Lai incident, and service-club financial scandals, one might well ask, "Why should a man of intellectual ability and moral integrity 'willingly imprison his gifts in such a calling'?"

Quality, Attributes, and Attitudes

In our current American society, where military-related issues have surfaced simultaneously with a general questioning of all authority and a relatively automatic reaction by our youth to any representatives of the "Establishment," the very nature and practice of the military hierarchical structure is being seriously questioned. It would seem to follow reasonably that if the intellect and general competence of an officer are questionable, then so might be the orders he issues and the policies he promulgates.

Samuel Huntington, in his excellent study, *The Soldier and the State*, examines the so-called "military mind" in terms of (1) its ability or quality, (2) its attributes or characteristics, and (3) its attitudes or substance (values and views). Today, how are military men likely to be judged against Huntington's criteria?

We can find a variety of views on their intellectual ability. The general conception is almost a stereotype from movies, television series, and popular novels. Everybody knows that military men don't think—they obey orders. ("Theirs not to reason why.") And of course there is a clear inverse ratio between rank and intellectual perceptiveness—the higher the rank, the lower the intellectual quality. The general conception is not very complimentary. A remarkably different view from a different era may be found in von Clausewitz, who held that the best of military leaders are not merely intelligent—in the sphere of areas relevant to war they are *geniuses*. But this view is in contrast to the attitude of the Prussian General Staff after 1860, which was that "genius is superfluous, even dangerous." They held that "reliance must be placed on average men succeeding by superior education, organization, and experience."

With respect to its attributes or characteristics, Huntington suggests general agreement that the military mind is thought to be "disciplined, rigid, logical, scientific; it is not flexible, tolerant, intuitive, emotional." I will return to these characteristics—especially discipline—later.

There are a number of general conceptions about the attitudes or substance of the military mind. It is thought to be antidemocratic, warlike and authoritarian, favoring aggression in foreign policy, believing that conflict and war develop man's highest moral and intellectual qualities, and believing that war is inevitable. In Fred Cook's attack on the military-industrial complex (*The Warfare State*), we are told that military men belong to the Radical Right, that they want war, even at the risk of total annihilation, and that they have joined forces with big industry in a combine driven by mutual self-interest and often in direct opposition to the nation's welfare and the ideal of international peace.

The least attractive picture of a power-mad military elite is easier to believe if one receives the kind of letter I did prior to the 1964 presidential election. It was signed by a retired Army brigadier general and declared that the "total elections of 1964" were "null and void." The author advocated that we "throw the rascals out" in vigilante fashion, and the writer declared himself ready "to lead the drive for the full restoration of Constitutional Government." He signed himself as Administrator of the Constitutional Provisional Government of the United States.

Was this a ridiculous hoax? Was the author of this letter mentally unbalanced? Incredible as it may seem, some Americans believe that such a letter represents accurately the current qualities and attitudes of the military mind. Some even believe that "it could happen here" (see the last installment of Khrushchev's memoirs).

Discipline, Creativity, and Moral Character

The aspect of military life at once both indispensable and the cause of much confusion about the "military mind" is *discipline*. There is abroad the illogical but not totally unwarranted view that the man accustomed to taking orders cannot be a creative thinker. The time-honored dictum that to give orders a man must first demonstrate that he is capable of following them is still observed in our military structure. And it ought to be. But is it not possible that by the time a man gets to be a general, he is so used to following orders that he no longer possesses the imagination and dynamism required of one who gives orders? Or as Galbraith now says in *How to Control the Military*, members of the military become so immersed in the bureaucracy that they are capable only of bureaucratic truth, which is parochial and always favors their own service and its defense-industry suppliers.

Murray Kempton, in reviewing Eisenhower's *Mandate for Change* in *The New Republic* (November 30, 1963), suggests that military discipline has a peculiar warping influence on moral character. He says:

> the good soldier will lie under orders as bravely as he will die under them. The garrison mind can produce acts that are honorable and even gallant; but notions of high virtue and selfless service seldom intrude upon it, being disposed of by discipline.

This thought—that discipline not only destroys creative thinking it "disposes of moral virtue—is even more disturbing than our previous one. Think of the impassioned pleas during the Nazi war-criminal trials: "I am not responsible!" "I was obeying orders!" "I acted as a soldier!" Certainly discipline can be a convenient scapegoat for abdicating moral responsibility. "Passing the buck" is a very ancient military game. It is also a very ancient human game.

We seem to have arrived at a rather unhappy dilemma. Everyone grants that discipline is essential to any military organization; yet some claim that discipline is incompatible with dynamic thinking. Others see it as an excuse for immoral behavior. By these measures, the man who devotes a lifetime to military service would seem to be both intellectually and morally insensitive. It is taken for granted that this same man is nevertheless very brave, very loyal, and so dedicated to the ideals of freedom and personal dignity that he is willing to risk his life in preserving these values for his countrymen. The stereotype begins to suggest a personality that can be easily duped, manipulated, and with little difficulty maneuvered into following some power-hungry leader in a military coup. We can add other characteristics to this "military mind," which further strengthen the possibility. Some say that the military mind is often conservative in the sense of fearing change, any change. It operates out of fear for the future (retirement pay, security, etc.) and hence will never rock the boat.

Are there really people like this in the military service? Yes. There are security-conscious, anti-intellectual, morally insensitive military men. There are also security-conscious, anti-intellectual, morally insensitive lawyers and doctors and politicians and plumbers. There are college professors who cling to old lectures, any old lectures; there are television repairmen who replace old tubes with other old tubes. But the crucial difference, the point we cannot afford to ignore, is that an irresponsible doctor or teacher may damage only a few lives, whereas an irresponsible military leader could conceivably destroy our whole way of life, if not human life itself.

If this stereotype of the military mind, which we have borrowed from various sources including our current literature, is a true picture of our military leaders, then we are truly in danger. And the scare-spreaders are quite right—it *could* happen here. There are *some* military officers who exhibit *some* of the characteristics of this stereotype. They are easy to single out precisely because they are different; they are *not* representative of the officer corps. There are, in fact, many great leaders in the military who are dynamic thinkers and doers and who have not had their moral standards "disposed of" by discipline.

Discipline, Responsibility, and Freedom

Let us examine discipline more closely. Just a little reflection should reveal that it is simply not true that discipline must destroy individual dynamism. Indeed, truly dynamic thinkers and leaders have and need great self-discipline. Plato, concerning himself with the proper training of those powerful intellects that should rule in the ideal "Republic," stressed the importance of the rigors of military discipline in preparing the philosopher-statesman for the intellectual tasks of a prospective ruler. It is important to note here that *appropriate* training in the external form of discipline, which is the military's stock in trade, is expected to assist in the development of individual self-discipline.

The central question has always been how to develop discipline without crushing creativity. What kind of character training can be blended with military training without destroying individual responsibility? Individual responsibility is universally assumed to be conjoined with individual freedom, which seems to be the direct antithesis of military discipline. In a recent address, "The Meaning of Freedom," William Pearson Tolley, President of Syracuse University, commented on the relationship between freedom and discipline on both the individual and social levels. On the individual level, he stated:

> it is the disciplined mind that is most truly free. We have always understood the power of a disciplined mind. What is not so clearly seen is the freedom that comes with this power. Man's triumphant journey to the moon is only the latest case in point. One can pay

> tribute to the level of American science and technology and particularly to the computers that multiply man's mathematical powers. What is more significant, however, is the self-discipline, dedication, and skill of the large company of men responsible for this magnificent achievement. The astronauts themselves are the visible heroes, but there are countless others like them. All are in the sharpest contrast to so many in our affluent society who appear alienated, aimless, undisciplined, and driven by impulse and emotion.

Looking at this dichotomy, one is struck not only by the contrast in life styles and values but in the sense of identity, and again in character and power. For our purposes, however, the significant contrast is in the exercise of freedom. The unskilled is not free. The uninstructed is not free. The inexperienced is not free. The undisciplined is not free. Whether the field is carpentry, athletics, or space technology, only the skilled, the instructed, the experienced, and the disciplined have both power and freedom.

On the social level, Tolley maintains further that "In a free society we seek order and justice as well as freedom, and these goals inevitably put a brake on personal freedom."

Tolley's views support the general proposition that the achievement of worthwhile goals is enhanced, not hindered, by discipline. The external disciplinary structure imposed by the military should not be motivated by the goal of limiting personal freedom but rather by the need to coordinate, order, and organize the efforts of large groups of men as they tackle the diverse tasks coincident to the defense of our way of life. The "brake" that military discipline applies to personal freedom is apparent, but it is at least analogous to the brake each individual applies to his appetites and emotions in order to accomplish any worthwhile task. Both forms of discipline are justifiable in terms of the order required to accomplish our goals. In this sense, Tolley seems to have hit it just right; with respect to goal accomplishment, "the undisciplined is not free."

But, one must still ask, what of personal responsibility and intellectual creativity in the restrictive context of the military structure? How shall we strike an appropriate balance? The answer lies in our willingness to nurture creative abilities and to encourage critical analysis within the system.

Striking a Balance

It is easy to encourage intellectual curiosity, analysis, and creativity in classrooms. It is not so easy, but even more important, to retain that questioning approach and scholarly attitude toward military training. If better ways of training can be found, then they should be adopted. If some practices can be shown to be purposeless, then better practices should replace them. But innovators must be prepared to accept responsibility when their innovations fail, as well as credit when they succeed. The crucial point, the crux of the balance we seek, is reached precisely when the time for research and questioning reaches its limit and a decision must be made.

In John Locke's phrase, citizens of a free society have consented to "be concluded by the majority" when decisions are reached. Socrates argued that when a man fails to persuade his government to change its policies, then he must either abide by them or leave the state. The military as an institution cannot escape an analogous position if it is to function well or even function at all. In a world where the men who wear uniforms are highly educated and where creativity is indeed nourished, there is room for discussion and contributions from those who are concerned enough and able enough. But when the contributions are all evaluated and the decisions are made, then military men are obliged to obey the orders of their superiors, just as ordinary citizens are obliged to abide by the laws of the state. In either case, other alternatives seem to lead inevitably to chaos.

The question of unlawful or immoral orders also is analogous to the question of illegitimate or unjust laws. Citizens are not obliged to obey laws that are clearly against the common good, or immoral in some other way. Similarly, soldiers are not obliged to obey orders that are clearly unlawful. Difficulties arise in those cases when either the legitimacy or the morality of the law or order is not clear, often because all of the relevant facts are not known.

In a democratic society, the ordinary citizen, who is unable to ascertain all of the facts, is willing to reside his trust in his elected representatives who do have the facts, or he attempts to elect officials he can trust. Soldiers analogously must place their trust in their military and civilian leaders. This kind of trust is not necessarily identical with the "unquestioning obedience" implied in the famous line quoted earlier, "Theirs not to reason why." Rather, in our time, it is clear that "unquestioning" obedience is a completely unacceptable, if not inappropriate, conception. Sophisticated, creative, dynamic men, whether in uniform or not, cannot be properly characterized as "unquestioning."

This is not the same as saying such men will not be obedient. Rather, if they are truly mature, responsible, and creative, they will have accepted the ultimate necessity of right order, and their willingness to obey is better characterized as *enlightened* obedience. When leaders do consult their men as a matter of course, when they do accept the ideas of others, when they do explain the reasons for various policies, then, in crisis situations, subordinates will indeed be justified in accepting orders immediately. Their trust, in this sense, is enlightened and justified.

It is not likely that those young officers who have both the noble aspirations and the requisite abilities to "do things better" will always get their ideas adopted. We noted that in the analogous case, the free citizen strives to elect other officials. For the young officer a more direct method is available, but it requires the patience to make small gains at each level in the hierarchy until he reaches a high enough position in the rank structure to achieve broad applications of his ideas. The new generation of officers can bring about changes in the old—and today the old are listening. To paraphrase William James, we are in the position of marrying new facts and new ideas to old and reliable values. Older officers are justifiably concerned that the reliable values might be set aside; the younger are justifiably concerned that their new ideas might not obtain a fair hearing.

Neither intellectual brilliance alone nor moral character and discipline alone will sustain us in our most desperate hours. We must not settle for less than an appropriate balance of the best of each.

Chapter 7

THE ETHICS OF LEADERSHIP I

Western world literature is replete with references to the normal qualities supposedly inherent in or at least inextricably associated with the profession of arms. From Thucydides and Plato to writings associated with Nuremberg and the My Lai and Lavelle affairs, emphasis has been placed on discerning the moral responsibilities of individuals within the constraints of bureaucratic disciplinary structures. Fixing responsibility in these circumstances is not simple because the relationship between human values and the military function is so intricate and complex. It will be my purpose in this chapter to examine that complexity with two major concerns in mind: an attempt, first, to understand the relationship between ethics and military leadership, and second, to venture some normative proposals concerning that relationship.

Ethos, Ethics, and Military Honor

Considerable confusion concerning ethics and military leadership is generated by the varying employment of terms like "military honor," "the military ethos," "the military ethic," "the military mind," "professionalism," "the military way," and so on. When Alfred Vagts provided his definition of "the military way" he seemed to have in mind a prescription of the "true" military function which would clearly distinguish the military role from the abuses of militarism. His definition appears devoid of value terms: "The military way is marked by a primary concentration of men and materials on winning specific objectives of power with the utmost efficiency, that is, with the least expenditure of blood and treasure. It is limited in scope, confined to one function, and scientific in its essential qualities."[1] However, as soon as Vagts begins to discuss the distinction between militarism and the military way, he finds himself involved immediately in a number of value questions, e.g., "humane use of materials and forces;" misuse of power, self-perpetuation, placing the military above the interest of the nation-state, and so on. It is important to point out that while it is possible to discuss meaningfully the "scientific" character of the military function per se, that characterization does not remove the essential moral tone

Reprinted from the *American Behavioral Scientist* 19, (May/June 1976). Reprinted with permission of the publisher, Sage Publications, Inc. Reprinted in a variety of publications including Wakin, M.M., ed., *War, Morality, and the Military Profession* (Boulder, Colo.: Westview Press, 1979, 1986).

of the military function. This point needs critical examination since there are many who would argue that the military function and hence the military leadership charged with carrying out that function, when viewed from the point of view of professional competence, must be considered morally neutral.

Perhaps one of the most extremely expressed opposing views is that voiced by Dean Acheson in a speech bearing on the use of military force. Acheson said:

> Those involved in the Cuban crisis of October, 1962, will remember the irrelevance of the supposed moral considerations brought out in the discussions. Judgment centered about the appraisal of dangers and risks, the weighing of the need for decisive and effective action against considerations of prudence; the need to do enough, against the consequences of doing too much. Moral talk did not bear on the problem. Nor did it bear upon the decision of those called upon to advise the president in 1949 whether and with what degree of urgency to press the attempt to produce a thermonuclear weapon. A respected colleague advised me that it would be better that our nation and people should perish rather than be party to a course so evil as producing that weapon. I told him that on the Day of Judgment his view might be confirmed and that he was free to go forth and preach the necessity for salvation. It was not, however, a view which I could entertain as a public servant.[2]

One plausible interpretation of Acheson's statement is that those military leaders providing advice to civilian policy makers need not concern themselves with ethical issues since the only relevant considerations are practical, not moral. Lieutenant General Sir John Winthrop Hackett provides a definition of the military function which might well fit Acheson's view, yet Hackett draws a profoundly opposite conclusion regarding the relationship of the moral to the military. Hackett suggests that the legitimate military function is "to furnish to a constituted authority . . . in situations where force is, or might be, used the greatest possible number of options." But those options are not devoid of moral considerations. Hackett affirms several times in different lectures that the principal task of the military today may well be to avoid war, the military function evolving to "the containment of violence" and not merely "the management of violence."[3] He says, "War in the sense of general unrestricted war, however, can no longer be regarded as a normal continuation of foreign policy or an alternative to peace."[4] Again he states, "War, total war, we have to avoid."[5]

Hackett, perhaps more than most other writers on this topic, emphasizes the intimate relationship between the moral and the functional aspects of the "military virtues." Hackett holds the eminently sound view that while loyalty, courage, and fortitude may well be and are desirable virtues in other walks of life, they are critically indispensable to the military function.[6] He further states that "the major service of the military institution to the community of men it serves may well lie neither within the political sphere nor the functional. It could easily lie within the moral."[7] We shall find occasion to return to this notion as we pursue in more detail the role of ethical considerations in military leadership. At this point we may wish to admit that an extension of the Acheson view previously cited is a possible description of the relationship between moral considerations and military advice (namely, that moral values are irrelevant); nevertheless, I shall attempt to show that such a strong involvement between the moral and the military exists and/or ought to exist from a normative point of view that the moral neutrality position must become untenable.

Those who use terms like "the military ethos" or "the military ethic" may have a slightly broader interpretation in mind than does Vagts when he refers to "the military way." I take "ethos" and "ethic" to be relatively synonymous collective references to the way of life and perspectives of the professional military leader. In modeling "the professional military ethic," Samuel Huntington attempts to characterize a relatively timeless view of "(1) basic values and perspectives, (2) national military policy, and (3) the relation of the military to the state." His justification for including any elements as part of this idealized ethic is "relevance to the performance of the military function."[8] Thus the function of the military profession implies a Hobbesian view of human nature that is weak, egoistic, savage, permanent, and prone to conflict. Further, success in war depends critically on subordination of the individual to the group. The military ethic is "fundamentally anti-individualistic"; in this realm we may find the strongest difference between the military value system and that of a liberal civilian society which stresses the importance and rights of the individual.

With respect to national military policy, Huntington's version of the military ethic is that it must view the nation-state as primary; it stresses the external threats to military security; it emphasizes the magnitude and the immediacy of the threats; it must favor strong, diverse, and ready military forces; it opposes international commitments and entry into war unless victory is assured. In discussing the relationship of the military and the state, Huntington holds that the professional ethic must view war as an instrument of politics and the military as the instrument of the state. The supremacy of civilian control is critical to the ethic. This leads to consideration of loyalty and obedience which Huntington calls the highest of the military virtues. Because of their importance, I shall postpone consideration of these virtues to a subsequent section of this paper and continue this section with some reflections on the concept of "military honor."[9]

The notion of military honor seems considerably more narrow than that of the professional military ethos or ethic. As Janowitz (1960) has pointed out, the belief system of all but the very elite military leaders may be more directly associated with the narrower notion of professional honor than with concern for political ideologies or more comprehensive views of a military ethic as depicted by Huntington.[10] My concern is that too narrow a view of honor has led to peculiar behavior patterns by military professionals in the past, and, in some ways, this narrow view continues to generate confusion and distortion. In the Western world we can find roots of the contemporary view of military honor in the aristocratic traditions of early European armies. Alfred Vagts relates the story of those peasants of southern Germany who fought for their emperor in 1078 against knights of the feudal armies who, upon defeating the peasants, castrated them for daring to bear arms, a privilege reserved for the aristocratic knights. Military honor, as characterized by Vagts, involved the practices of chivalry, including duels, but extended only to aristocratic peers.[11] Janowitz suggests that the "code" of military honor in the military was inherited from the British and contained the following four components: (1) officers are gentlemen, (2) personal loyalty is owed to the commander, (3) officers are members of one big brotherhood, and (4) officers fight for traditional glory.[12]

Modification of this code in the contemporary U.S. military is obvious. While we find American officers still concerned about being "gentlemen," that term refers today to standards of behavior and officer responsibilities rather than to aristocratic birth. Chivalry has generally survived only in attempts to provide appropriate treatment for prisoners of war. It is no longer the case that extreme value is placed on personal loyalty to a commander; that aspect of military honor is transferred to the oath of office which requires allegiance to the Constitution and to the position rather than the person of the president as commander in chief. The notion of brotherhood remains a strong component of the concept of military honor. It is still a matter of pride for many professionals to point out that "an officer's word is his bond" and it is a continual source of annoyance to many that they should be required to supply identification cards or driver's licenses or any references other than the fact that they are military officers if they should wish to cash a check or require credit. But the notion of group unity and brotherhood is most emphatically felt in what Janowitz calls "a single overriding directive": the professional soldier always fights. To refuse a combat assignment is to commit the most serious offense against one's military honor and to break faith with one's peers. As for the fourth component of military honor, we must agree with Janowitz that "contemporary military honor repudiates the glory of war." Perhaps we have substituted for the pursuit of glory the perception that the military life is a rugged and strenuous life of service to the state demanding personal sacrifice.

But discussion of "military honor" in its classical setting does not do justice to the complex uses of the concept of "honor" as it relates to military leadership. Many military leaders first associated honor with military life through their exposure to honor codes at the service academies. Certainly there has been sufficient publicity in recent years to generate curiosity about, opposition to, defense of, and emotional responses to the employment of these codes. Such codes have been characterized as too stringent when compared to the value standards of the present society from which the service academy students come (this criticism seems to have been ameliorated considerably since the Watergate affair and the alleged false reporting associated with the highly publicized case of General Lavelle). Administration of the codes has been criticized, particularly as regards the maturity of the student honor committees and the legal protection afforded those who are accused of honor violations. But a more important issue to examine should be the question of the lasting perception of honor that experience with an honor code provides to military leaders.

Codes of conduct, whether they be framed as honor codes for service academies, moral commandments for religious groups, prescriptions for medical or legal practitioners, and so on, all seem subject to the same sort of narrow interpretation which may cause distortions in our general view of moral behavior. The immature or unsophisticated frequently narrow their ethical sights to the behavior specifically delineated in the code so that what may have originally been intended as a minimum listing becomes treated as an exhaustive guide for ethical action. We forget all too easily the wisdom concerning these matters given us by almost every moral philosopher dating back at least as far as Socrates, Plato, or Aristotle. The classical Greek conception of the just or honorable man encompassed all of one's human acts. Moral prescriptions are given in broad terms, e.g., "seek the golden mean of moderation between the extremes of too much and too little" or "act in accordance with right reason." Aristotle would advise us not to seek more precision than our subject matter permits; moral philosophy cannot provide the specific conclusions of a mathematical system. We can identify general classes of good and bad human actions, e.g., promise-keeping, truth-telling, lying, cheating, stealing, and so on; but the crucial step to right behavior is not following a rule because it is a rule. Rather one becomes a good man through performing good actions. The critical thing is what kind of person one becomes in the long run, throughout a lifetime. Perhaps as far back as the sixth century B.C., Lao Tzu, the alleged founder of ancient Taoism, expressed this view of mankind's moral goal in the saying, "The way to do is to be."

The honor codes at the service academies single out lying, cheating, stealing (and tolerating these actions by peers) as act-types which are strictly proscribed with severe penalties (usually dismissal) for those who engage in these actions. In a real sense, this suggests a very Aristotelian approach to character development. If one practices telling the truth all the time—if one refrains from cheating and stealing all of the time—then these actions may well become part of the habitual human response to one's environmental circumstances. Such a person's character may be described as truthful and honest. But the avoidance of lying, cheating, and stealing does not by itself encompass all that we mean when we judge a person to be honorable.

At least one of the academies (the Air Force Academy) has a separate committee called an ethics committee which is concerned with cadet behavior not specifically included in the honor code. The existence of separate committees may lead the immature into an erroneous separation of "honorable" behavior from "ethical" behavior. Further, this same unsophisticated perception has yet to account for "moral" behavior, which some view as the very narrow "personal" area of sexual conduct which is somehow outside the realm of honor or ethics. Perhaps I have pursued this extreme distortion of views of honor, ethics, and morality much further than warranted by existing perceptions. However, we have occasionally had placed before us images of military leaders (often fictional heroes) whose private conduct (sexual, social, and so on) seems to function on a totally different level from their public conduct or their functioning in their areas of "professional competence." One thinks of the parallel with the age of chivalry in which the courtesies involved in the "rules" of chivalric conduct were extended only to one's peers but did not apply to behavior in other contexts or with other persons. It would seem rather ironic if the extreme separation of human acts into these artificially distinguished categories—the honorable, the ethical, and the moral—were to find some beginnings for military leaders in the very institutions which place profound stress on the development of the "whole man." And how would such category distinctions affect the advice of a Plato or an Aristotle who would recommend to the young who might aspire to military and moral leadership to "find a good man and imitate him"? The strange notion that honor is public but morality is private will receive further attention.

Obedience

As was noted previously, Huntington tells us that "loyalty and obedience are the highest military virtues," and Hackett pointed out that these virtues are absolutely critical to the military function. Huntington quotes Alfred T. Mahan on this point: "The rule of obedience is simply the expression of that one among the military virtues upon which all the others depend."[13] Huntington places before us such a strict view of military obedience that it is worth reproducing here for commentary.

> When the military man receives a legal order from an authorized superior, he does not argue, he does not hesitate, he does not substitute his own views; he obeys instantly. He is judged not by the policies he implements, but rather by the promptness and efficiency with which he carries them out. His goal is to perfect an instrument of obedience; the uses to which that instrument is put are beyond his responsibility. His highest virtue is instrumental not ultimate. Like Shakespeare's soldier in *Henry V* he believes that the justice of the

> cause is more than he should "know" or "seek after." For if the king's "cause be wrong, our obedience to the King wipes the crime of it out of us."[14]

This statement of the military ideal is slightly softened by noting that it begins with reference to legal orders from authorized superiors. Huntington himself goes on to discuss the limits of military obedience. But the latter part of the quotation above presents us with an issue concerning military leadership that requires much consideration. Telford Taylor has performed an excellent service in summarizing American and international law and court decisions regarding lawful orders and the responsibilities of military subordinates and superiors.[15] He directs our attention to *The Law of Land Warfare* where the following statement of American law is found: "The fact that the law of war has been violated pursuant to an order of a superior authority, whether military or civil, does not deprive the act in question of its character as a war crime, nor does it constitute a defense in the trial of an accused individual, unless he did not know and *could not reasonably have been expected to know* that the act ordered was unlawful."[16]

The emphasis on instant obedience and total loyalty to the military ideal of subordination to military superiors and civilian leaders is critical and appropriate. An enlisted man in a battle context may well be unable to examine battle orders for legality. But the military professional, the officer leader, ought in fact "to seek after" the "justice of the cause." Obedience to orders is not in itself either a legal or a moral claim of right action, although it is certainly a mitigating circumstance. Military leaders cannot be *merely* instrumental to the state. They are instrumental, yes; but they must at the same time accept a portion of the responsibility for the uses of the military instrument. How else, without investigating the issues involved, could any military leader ever make a decision concerning the legality or morality of his orders? Our current laws say that if he could reasonably be expected to know that his orders were not lawful, then "obedience to the King" could not remove the crime from his own responsibility.

It is clear from the behavior of some military officers as well as from some of their public statements that it is possible to divorce oneself from moral considerations altogether and insist that the contractual nature of service to the state is *merely* legal. It is at the same time clear that this position fails to recognize that a freely given commitment generates one of the strongest moral claims against the person who gives it whether that commitment be to private individuals or to a larger segment of society. That commitments voluntarily given involve obligations to fulfill them is not easily proven, although it is easily seen. On utilitarian grounds alone one can establish that fulfillment of commitments made must lead to a better ordered universe and provide for the greater good of society than nonfulfillment. On Kantian grounds one easily sees that promise-keeping is the kind of human act that can be universalized and that keeping one's word involves treating other human beings as ends-in-themselves, beings with dignity whose worth is recognized when our commitments to them are honored. The military leader who does not accept this fundamental approach to the moral relevance of his oath of office may do many things well but he will not command the respect or loyalty of his subordinates.

Even Thomas Hobbes (1651) observed that once one enters into a contractual agreement with others (the state), one has accepted the fulfillment of his part of the agreement as a moral obligation; indeed, Hobbes defines injustice as the breaking of one's contractual agreements.[17] If one is morally bound to keep his promises, then he takes on a *moral* commitment to obey the orders of his superiors when he takes the military oath of office just as the marriage promise constitutes a moral commitment even though it too takes the form of a legal contract. Thus obedience to orders is not merely a functional expedient for military men; it involves at the same time a moral commitment. The ground rules for violating this moral commitment are subject to the same considerations as are relevant to other moral contexts: we are justified in violating one of our moral obligations just when that obligation is in conflict with another, higher obligation and the circumstances are such that we cannot fulfill both. This principle, of course, involves critical normative considerations to which we will return.

That there are limits to military obedience can be readily granted; what these limits are is not so easily determined, precisely because obedience is so critical to the military function. Huntington's discussion of these limits is excellent. He points out that military obedience can conflict with the aims of professional competence when a subordinate perceives that the orders received will not accomplish the superior's objectives or when rigid adherence to past ways of doing things does not permit new ideas to develop. Huntington expresses these conflicts between military obedience and professional competence as issues of an officer's moral virtue versus his intellectual virtue. He further notes that there are at least four kinds of conflict which can arise between military obedience and nonmilitary values.[18] Military obedience may conflict with political wisdom as in the case of General MacArthur, who disagreed with the policies laid down by his civilian political superiors for prosecuting the Korean War. Military obedience may conflict also when civilian leaders dictate military strategy which supposedly rests within the professional competence of the military leaders. Further conflicts with military obedience include the obvious cases of legality and morality. The case of Lieutenant Calley and My Lai certainly involved the intertwined questions of obedience to orders versus both the legality and the morality of these orders concerning the treatment of prisoners.

Much attention has been given recently to the ethical responsibilities of military officers on this complex issue of conflict with the military ideal of obedience. In the *Congressional Record-Senate* some interesting commentary on this subject is made, principally by Senator Hughes of Iowa.[19] His remarks were made in the context of Senate hearings regarding the nominations for promotion of general officers, two of whom were air force officers who had previously been in General John D. Lavelle's chain of command in Southeast Asia during the period that General Lavelle was accused of ordering falsified reports of bombing strikes which violated the written rules of agreement. Senator Hughes opposed the promotion of these two officers on the grounds that they should have questioned General Lavelle's orders but did not. His view is that military leaders remain responsible for insuring that the law of the land is carried out and are not permitted merely to accept the orders of an immediate superior when that order is known to conflict with national policy and written directives from the Joint Chiefs of Staff. Some of Senator Hughes' remarks that bear relevance for our consideration of the complex role of obedience follow:

> I could not rest easy if I thought that one of these men who knowingly participated in this false reporting might one day become chairman of the Joint Chiefs of Staff. The integrity of our command and control structure, both within the military and under civilian authority, depends upon men of the highest character, whose obedience to our laws and the Constitution is unquestioned. . . . If we choose to reward these men with promotions, what will the consequences be? . . . Will the officers down the line conclude that loyalty and obedience within one's service are more important than adherence to the higher principles of law and civilian control of the military? [20]

General John D. Ryan, former Air Force Chief of Staff, issued a policy letter to his commanders, subsequent to the Lavelle incident, regarding the relationship between integrity and command. It is clear that the ideal which General Ryan proposes places the value of integrity above unquestioning obedience of commands; indeed, he makes integrity the *sine qua non* of the military command structure:

> Integrity—which includes full and accurate disclosure—is the keystone of military service. . . In any crisis decisions and risks taken by the highest national authorities depend, in large part, on reported military capabilities and achievements. In the same way every commander depends on accurate reporting from his forces. . . . Therefore, we may not compromise our integrity—our truthfulness. To do so is not only unlawful but degrading. False reporting is a clear example of a failure of integrity. Any order to compromise integrity is not a lawful order. Integrity is the most important responsibility of command. Commanders are dependent on the integrity of those reporting to them in every decision they make.

> Integrity can be ordered but it can only be achieved by encouragement and example.[21]

We are reminded of Hackett's view that while some moral qualities are merely desirable in other walks of life, they may be absolutely imperative for the military function. Integrity would appear to be one of those critical moral qualities which makes loyalty and obedience possible. In this sense Mahan may need to be corrected: integrity rather than obedience may well be "that one among the military virtues upon which all of the others depend."

There have been a plethora of stories concerning false body counts reported in Vietnam. Lieutenant Colonel M. T. Smith details further inaccurate reporting in such areas as aircraft equipment status reports, aircraft accident reports, and general military training requirements.[22] Smith attributes much of the inaccurate (euphemism for "false") reporting to two major aspects of current institutional reality: our stated goals are so high as to appear unrealistic, and some leaders give bad examples. There are high-ranking officers who do not take bad news well, so members of their staffs frequently tell their bosses just what they want to hear. "It is difficult to expect integrity from the rank and file if the rank and file do not see that same quality in those who lead them."[23] According to Smith, our stated goals for such things as aircraft operationally ready rates and repair cycle rates have on occasion been unrealistic; and out of fear, competent people have simply not reported truthfully that those rates were not being met. Smith's suggested solutions to inaccurate reporting involve total emphasis on integrity for every leader and adjustment of management systems to provide more realistic, achievable goals which are mission oriented. A recent empirical "Study on Military Professionalism" requested by General Westmoreland and produced by the Army War College verifies that in the army, as well as in the air force, management systems have sometimes emphasized the development of statistical results at the high cost of diluting the quality of moral leadership. Indeed a summary description from the U.S. Army War College study strikes a remarkable parallel with the situation described by Smith:

> A scenario that was repeatedly described in seminar sessions and narrative responses includes an ambitious, transitory commander—marginally skilled in the complexities of his duties—engulfed in producing statistical results, fearful of personal failure, too busy to talk with or listen to his subordinates, and determined to submit acceptably optimistic reports which reflect faultless completion of a variety of tasks at the expense of the sweat and frustration of his subordinates.[24]

The Army War College study is well done. It utilizes a data base generated from questionnaires administered to 420 relatively elite officers from six different service schools (69 percent of them were lieutenant colonels and colonels) and twenty-five seminar discussions with a total of 250 officers including a much larger percentage of captains and majors. One general finding was the large number of strong perceptions of a marked "disharmony between traditional, accepted ideals and the prevailing institutional pressures." The traditional ideals are briefly summed up in the phrase "duty, honor, country." The study concludes that there has been little change in officers' perceptions of the professional ethical ideals but that the current institutional climate (not changes in civil society at large) is largely responsible for the perceived failure of many officers to live up to those ideals. High on the list of possible institutional causal factors for unethical behavior is the demand for perfection: "Faultless performance may be a suitable immediate goal for production line workers who have routine tasks or for skilled technicians who have nearly infinite time. For those who deal with complex organizations, changing missions, and people of various aptitudes, perfection or 'zero defects' is an impossibility."[25]

In exploring the relationship between "ethical behavior" and "military competence" as viewed by the officers in their sample, the Army War College study found the two concepts to be so closely intertwined that "inadequate performance in one area contributes to inadequate performance in the other."[26] In general, the War College study confirms the view already expressed in various ways in this chapter that ethical values are absolutely critical to the function of military leadership. If the present climate in the services can itself be viewed as generating a deterioration of those moral values, then it must also be viewed as hindering rather than facilitating the prosecution of the military function. The study suggested the following consequences of the army's present (1970) climate:

> It is conducive to self-deception because it fosters the production of inaccurate information; it impacts on the long-term ability of the army to fight and win because it frustrates young, idealistic, energetic officers who leave the service and are replaced by those who will tolerate if not condone ethical imperfection; it is corrosive of the army's image because it falls short of the traditional idealistic code of the soldier—a code which is the key to the soldier's acceptance by a modern free society; it lowers the credibility of our top military leaders because it often shields them from essential bad news; it stifles initiative, innovation, and humility because it demands perfection or the pose of perfection at every turn; it downgrades technical competence by rewarding instead trivial, measurable, quota-filling accomplishments; and it eventually squeezes much of the inner satisfaction and personal enjoyment out of being an officer.[27]

It is certainly a tenable thesis that the structure of an institution that depends critically on the acceptance of obedience as one of its highest values may place a strain on the moral integrity of its members. But structures are ultimately molded by individuals; and those individuals charged with the responsibility of guiding the institution can, if they have the wisdom and will to do so, revise institutional pressures so that they become supportive of a healthy relationship between integrity and obedience and minimize possible conflicts which could arise between these essential attributes of the military leadership function.

Some Normative Considerations

In *The Professional Soldier,* Janowitz distinguished between "absolutists" and "pragmatists" regarding orientations of military leaders toward international relations. Janowitz did not interpret these conceptions in terms of personal moral values per se but restricted his discussion to the differing perceptions of the role of war; e.g., the absolute school, which was viewed as growing out of the punitive expedition tradition, views war as the basis of international relations and generally accepts no substitute for victory. The pragmatic school on the other hand views war as only one component of international relations and is more likely to think of furthering political objectives by the "right amount" of military force.[28] The absolutists are more likely to believe in major atomic warfare than the pragmatists. Because "absolutism" and "pragmatism" are more commonly used in their broader applications to human values and are frequently used to characterize the personal value systems of military leaders, I should like to enter into some fundamental considerations of these conceptions.

Those military officers who are viewed as moral absolutists are often called "men of high principle" and "uncompromising." Those viewed as pragmatists are often associated with "expediency" or "flexibility." Either of these characterizations is viewed as praiseworthy or pejorative depending upon the context and the persons employing them. To be flexible is sometimes to be mature and sophisticated; to be accused of expediency is sometimes equivalent to being accused of being unethical. Analogously, to be uncompromising is sometimes to be narrow and stubborn and unsophisticated; on the other hand, a leader who is unwilling to compromise his absolute principles is sometimes viewed as noble. I maintain that most of us are very fuzzy in our thinking about moral absolutes and their alternatives in a fashion parallel to the confusion mentioned earlier regarding honor, ethics, and personal morality.

In making the distinction between absolutism and pragmatism we seem to imply that the two conceptions represent exhaustive opposing categories, that one holds either one of these positions or the other. Further, because of our general predilections for simplicity, we often rest with the notion that the only alternative to absolutism is relativism; and hence pragmatism and relativism in ethics must be identical.[29] It is a very easy step from these popular conceptions to conclude that a military officer who subscribes to absolute moral principles may well be so inflexible as to demand and give unquestioning obedience in every context. Analogously, those who do not subscribe to the absolute character of moral principles are easily viewed as relativists, either in the cultural or the subjective sense. That this simple bifurcation is inaccurate is easily seen if we attempt to define carefully what is meant by an absolute moral principle or an absolute obligation. If we maintain that an absolute obligation is one that holds with no exceptions for all human beings and in all possible sets of circumstances, then many will argue that there are no such obligations which could be morally binding. But there are. For example, "One ought always to seek to do good and avoid evil" is an absolute obligation in the sense defined. So is "One ought always to act in accordance with right reason." Immediately we see something very important to notice about absolutes characterized in this fashion: the more human actions we attempt to incorporate under a single principle, the less specific the principle can be; absolute moral principles are necessarily vague. Further we should note that if principles really are absolute in the sense defined above, they could never be in conflict with each other since each must be obeyed in all possible circumstances.

Clearly, those moral obligations dealing with human act-types, like truth-telling, promise-keeping, preservation of life, respect for the property of others, and so on, are not absolute obligations. Does that mean that they are relative obligations to be observed only when we find it expedient to do so? Certainly not. Rather it is the case that we could best refer to these types of moral obligations by use of another term; for the moment, let us call them "universal" obligations. How are they different from either absolute or relative principles? Ought they always to be observed? No. Then they cannot be absolutes. Can they conflict? Yes. Then they cannot be absolutes. Are they sufficiently arbitrary to be ignored whenever one is in a different society or whenever it is convenient or expedient to do so? No. Then they cannot be relative principles in either the cultural or most subjective sense. Universal obligations of this sort hold for all human beings (they are not subjectively or culturally relative) but not in all possible circumstances (they are not absolute). They hold in analogous sets of circumstances and they may conflict with each other.

An easy example may help clarify the nature and status of universal obligations. Suppose we agree that we have a universal obligation to keep our promises and also a universal obligation to preserve human life whenever it is in our power to do so. Suppose further we have promised to meet our commanding officer for lunch at the officers club and we depart in sufficient time to keep our commitment but en route we encounter an automobile accident with a victim screaming for help. Shall we stop? Of course we will stop even though to do so will mean breaking our promise. In this particular case, simple as it is, we see immediately that the obligation to attempt to preserve life is higher than the obligation to keep a promise in these particular circumstances. Other circumstances might demand a different moral judgment. The role that circumstances or "situations" play is an important one when obligations conflict. Please note that the fact that we judged it morally permissible to break the promise in this case does not mean that we have given up the universal obligation to keep our promises. We still accept that obligation as strongly as ever. Our rule of action is that we are justified in violating our universal moral obligations only when they conflict with a higher obligation and we cannot fulfill both at once. Thus if one is torn between obedience to an order and fulfillment of another moral obligation, he or she must judge which is the higher obligation in those circumstances. Universal obligations are neither absolute nor relative. They bind all human beings in analogous sets of circumstances, but they may conflict. The larger question dealing with the source of these obligations must be dealt with on a philosophical level beyond the scope of this chapter.

"The Way to Do Is to Be"

Loyalty and obedience, integrity and courage, subordination of the self to the good of the military unit and the nation-state—these are among the moral virtues critical to the military function, and they take the form of universal obligations. Seen in this context, the moral tone must be pervasive for both public and private actions of the ideal military leader. These qualities are essential to the effective and appropriate functioning of all military people, but those who lead are most responsible for exemplifying them and inculcating them in others. Only a narrowly faulty view of the moral life could sustain the view that one must be honorable in his public duties but that one's private moral code might operate on some other level. Consider the inconsistency in a leader who might insist on truthful reporting but falsifies his personal income tax return. Consider also the leader who asks for trust and loyalty from his subordinates but is unfaithful to his wife on temporary duty trips. Narrow views of ethics will not do for one who aspires to effective military leadership. One's character is what counts and evaluations of character are all-encompassing.

Because the military function is so directly related to our highest human values, those charged with the leadership of that function must be sensitive to those values and must exhibit some understanding of them. The values of American society are said by many to be "liberal," yet the military services responsible for defending those liberal values are said themselves to be "conservative," for those who would defend the status quo are so labeled. Concern for the individual dignity of each person suggests a liberal orientation, while those who would fight to preserve individual dignity must be asked to sublimate in many ways their own individualism for the sake of the group. It is in this sense that contemporary commentators are wont to point out a paradoxical discrepancy between supposed civilian values and the military virtues. Yet, most acknowledge that without the conservative values of loyalty, obedience, and self-restraint, the military function would disintegrate. Hackett suggests that it is the responsibility of the military leader to bridge this seeming paradox when he reminds us that "the young officer . . . has to be made to remember that only a person of liberal mind is entitled to exercise coercion over others in a society of free men."[30] The authority of military superiors over their subordinates is stronger and more complete than that of almost any other human relationship in our societal structure. With that authority goes the frightening responsibility to respect the dignity of individual subordinates at the same time that military order and discipline are preserved. It is precisely in the person of the military leader that the liberal and the conservative values must be brought together in a daily attempt at fragile balance. It is not an easy thing that we ask of these leaders, but it is necessary.

In this context, how does a military leader inspire loyalty, the loyalty which leads one to accept enlightened obedience in an understanding way as a moral obligation in a military structure? In his excellent treatment of this topic, Captain Michael Wheeler suggests that loyalty is best engendered in subordinates when they can reside their full trust in their leaders and that trust itself is readily given only to those superiors who are perceived to be persons of high moral integrity.[31] How often we are driven back to this critical point! We must ask as much of our leaders as Tennyson attributed to the Duke of Wellington when he referred to him as "The statesman-warrior, moderate, resolute / Whole in himself, a common good."

Where military leadership has been less than ideal, it has faltered because of a faulty view of the whole man; it has seen the role of morality in military leadership too narrowly or from a relativistic framework. We ask of today's leader that he be neither absolutist nor relativist but retain a balanced perspective that understands the full complexity which characterizes the interweaving of moral value with military function. We ask him to be that good man, that wise man that the Greek philosopher could advise subordinates to find and imitate. Fully accepting the Aristotelian wisdom that moral character develops out of repeating good actions, that it cannot be ordered but can be exemplified and imitated, our advice to those who aspire to become worthy military leaders can be none other than that of the ancient Chinese sage: "The way to do is to be."

Notes

1. Alfred Vagts, *A History of Militarism* (New York: Free Press, 1959), 13.

2. Dean Acheson, "Ethics in International Relations Today," in *The Vietnam Reader*, edited by M. Raskin and B. Fall (New York: Random House, 1965), 13.

3. Sir John Winthrop Hackett (General), "The Military in the Service of the State" (Harmon Memorial Lecture, U.S. Air Force Academy, Colorado, 1970).

4. "Military in the Service of the State"

5. "Military in the Service of the State"

6. Sir John Winthrop Hackett (General), *The Profession of Arms* (London: Times Publishing, 1962), 45.

7. Hackett, "Military in the Service of the State."

8. Samuel P. Huntington, *The Soldier and the State* (New York: Random House, 1957), 62. Further delineation of Huntington's view of the professional military ethic is taken essentially from Chapter 3, which is descriptively entitled "The Military Mind: Conservative Realism of the Professional Military Ethic."

9. Huntington, 64-65.

10. Morris Janowitz, *The Professional Soldier* (New York: Free Press, 1960).

11. Vagts, "History of Militarism," 42.

12. Janowitz, *Professional Soldier,* 217.

13. Huntington, *Soldier and the State,* 73.

14. *Soldier and the State.*

15. Telford Taylor, *Nuremberg and Vietnam: An American Tragedy* (New York: Bantam, 1971).

16. U.S. Army, *The Law of Land Warfare,* U.S. Army Field Manual, Department of the Army, 1956, 182.

17. Thomas Hobbes, *Leviathan, 1651.*

18. Huntington, *Soldier and the State,* 74-78.

19. *Congressional Record-Senate,* 1974, 56257-56262.

20. *Senate*, 56258.

21.John D. Ryan (General), "Air Force Policy Letter for Commanders" Washington, D.C., 1 November 1972. General Ryan's view of integrity versus obedience starkly contrasts with that of Murray Kempton, who stated, "The good soldier will lie under orders as bravely as he will die under them." (Review of Eisenhower's *Mandate for Change, New Republic* [30 November 1963].)

22. M. T. Smith (Lieutenant Colonel), "Reporting Inaccuracies—a Rose by Another Name," *Air University Review, 1974.*

23. Smith, "Reporting Inaccuracies", 85.

24. U.S. Army War College, *Study on Military Professionalism* (Carlisle Barracks, Pa.: U.S. Army War College, 1970), 13-14.

25. *Study on Military Professionalism*, 24.

26. *Study on Military Professionalism*, 30-31.

27. *Study on Military Professionalism*, 29.

28. Janowitz, *Professional Soldier,* 272ff.

29. Chaplain Kermit D. Johnson (Colonel), "Ethical Issues of Military Leadership," *Parameters*, 4 (1974), 35-39. Chaplain Johnson makes an interesting comment on the relationship between "what works" and ethical relativism, suggesting

that the pragmatic outlook is in fact a "subtle and disguised form of ethical relativism practiced frequently in the military setting." Johnson identifies ethical relativism as one of four pressing issues concerning military leadership. The other three are the exaggerated loyalty syndrome, the obsession with image, and the drive for success.

30. Hackett, "Military in the Service of the State."

31. Michael O. Wheeler, "Loyalty, Honor, and the Modern Military," *Air University Review* (1973), 50-55.

Chapter 8

THE ETHICS OF LEADERSHIP II

A leader is best
When people barely know that he exists,
Not so good when people obey and acclaim him,
Worst when they despise him.
"Fail to honor people,
They fail to honor you,"
But of a good leader, who talks little,
When his work is done, his aim fulfilled,
They will all say, "We did this ourselves."
–Lao Tzu, sixth century B.C.;
Verse 17 of the *Tao Teh Ching*

It is possible to infer much more from this verse in the *Tao Teh Ching* concerning ethics and leadership than its author could have intended so many centuries ago. Lao Tzu saw human leadership at its best when it imitated the most harmonious ways of nature flowing smoothly like a natural stream, without harshness or aggressive struggle, and marked always by a gentleness that naturally pulled subordinates to their tasks. This is a view totally inimical to that of the leader as an egoistic order-giver who forces compliance from subordinates by threats and claims sole credit for any positive results of their efforts. With some trepidation, I would like to reflect on these two extreme characterizations of superior-subordinate relationships, pursuing a fundamental notion first suggested to me in a paper delivered by William May[1] and developing the ethical implications of adopting one mode of leadership rather than another. Following these reflections, I hope to be able to establish the critical importance of ethical considerations to military leadership in the light of the unique function of the military profession.

Reprinted from *Military Leadership*, edited by J.H. Buck and L.J. Korb (Beverly Hills, Calif: Sage Publications). Copyright 1981 by J.H. Buck. Also in Wakin, M.M., ed., *War, Morality, and the Military Profession*, Westview Press, 1986. Reprinted with permission.

Social Contract or Polity[2]

In the many criticisms of military leadership which have been published in recent years, much attention has been given to the image of a ruthless, ambitious careerist, intent upon furthering his own interests in his climb up the hierarchical ladder in spite of or even because of the high personal cost he may extract from contemporaries, subordinates, or the actual military mission itself. This is one of the anecdotal statements made by an Army major who was interviewed during the Army War College's research for their *Study on Military Professionalism:* "My superior was a competent, professional, knowledgeable military officer who led by fear, would doublecross anyone to obtain a star, drank too much and lived openly by no moral code. He is now a Brigadier General!"[3] But the "careerists" are not a peculiar military phenomena; they are to be found in many of our professions. And it is not as though ethical considerations are irrelevant for these professional climbers—they have an ethic, but as Max Lerner puts it, "It is the wrong one." Lerner refers to this ethic in contemporary business parlance as the "bottom line" ethic.

> For a politician, the ethic is to get power and hold on to it; for a lawyer, it is to win his case and get his fee . . . for a corporate executive, the ethic is to win out in the lethally competitive struggle for profits, markets, stock values. The bottom line is what counts, whatever the means used. It is the cancer of the professions.[4]

How does one find oneself caught up in this bottom-line ethic, not only without sensitivity for the means employed but often with the seeming conviction that promotion (the symbol of success) is evidence of virtue? The means employed "worked"; can there still be ethical questions to ask? Promotion itself provides vindication for the means employed. One possible explanation of the "ethic" is that it is an understandable extended outcome of a certain position on the nature of man, advocated in its most primitive form by Thomas Hobbes.

Hobbes is used as one of the classic representatives of egoism in most textbooks of moral philosophy. His view of man in the *Leviathan* begins with the assumption that all men are equal in the state of nature; that is, as they appear in the world considered apart from any formal social or political structure. In the primal condition, every man has an equal right to everything and moral terms have no meaning. There can be no right or wrong if every person has a right to everything; the fundamental rule of behavior involves personal survival by the use of one's own devices. This natural condition of man is chaotic, savage, and marked by violence. Indeed Hobbes tells us that "during the time men live without a common power to keep them all in awe, they are in that condition which is called war; and such a war, as is of every man, against every man." Life for man in such conditions is "solitary, poor, nasty, brutish, and short" (*Leviathan:* ch. 13). But man is also endowed with reason which ultimately leads him to conclude that if he is to survive, he must seek peace with other men. He must give up his right to harm other men if he can persuade them to do likewise and enter into an agreement, a social contract with them. However, the mere fact of the existence of an agreement does not change human nature. It is still the case that "of the voluntary acts of every man, the object is some *good to himself*" (*Leviathan:* ch. 14). So to guarantee that men will abide by their agreements, tremendous powers must be granted to government (the real leviathan) so that men will live up to their social contract out of fear of punishment. For the first time, moral terms have meaning once the agreement is made: Living up to the contract is "justice"; breaking it is injustice. All laws passed by the agreed-upon government become moral obligations: morality itself rests on the agreement—it is man-made and not found either in nature or in accordance with nature. Moral rules are legislated.

This brief elaboration of Hobbes's account of the nature of man and the origins of government through a social contract is relevant to any analysis of military leadership. The Hobbesian view of man is held by several commentators on the military profession to be essential to the military ethic.[5] This view might also be at the root of the moral comfortableness of the careerist mentioned previously. If self-interest is the primary focus of human action, or if, more to the point, it *ought* to be, then one may feel morally justified if hierarchical ambitions are realized even at high cost to others. Here, we may reflect on William May's suggestion that social contract theories "tracing the origin of the state to a supreme evil" (namely, man's predatory nature) give rise to adversary relationships on every side. May made specific reference to John Locke's version of the social contract theory rather than to that of Hobbes, perhaps because Locke is viewed as having more direct influence on the framers of the American Constitution. Locke, of course, did not share Hobbes's extreme egoistic view of man although he placed great stress on innate human rights, especially the right to private property. For both Hobbes and Locke, however, it seems accurate to conclude that governments are essentially founded in negative fashion to provide security to the individual from the threat posed by other men.

If one stops for a moment to place the Hobbesian contractual view into the context of the military profession, it is easy to develop the least attractive picture of military leadership. Orders can be seen as justified *because* the military leader gives them (he is authorized by contract to do so), not because they make sense or are appropriate to the task addressed. A legitimate answer to the query "Why?" on this analysis would always be, "Because the general said so." Further if Hobbes's version of psychological egoism were correct, one could hardly expect to find any examples of self-sacrifice or subordination of the good of the self to the good of the unit, service, or nation. And yet, if we analyze the critical and essential functions that are uniquely military (more on this later), we see immediately that self-sacrifice rather than self-interest is an essential ingredient both of military leadership and of military service in general. Self-interest theories of ethics and the view of human nature in which they are grounded are simply not appropriate for the military profession (nor indeed for any of the professions focused on service to the greater society).

In one sense, at least, the military profession is more akin to the classical Greek notion of polity than to the communities of the social contract theorists. The fundamental mission of the military under a constitutional government must be associated with the common good, the good of the community it serves. When the military or any branch of the military places its own interests ahead of the nation's overall interest, we soon see elements of the militarism that Alfred Vagts,[6] General Hackett,[7] and others have adequately described. Militarism is, as it were, careerism writ large, and both are grounded in the ethics of self-interest. In reflecting on Aristotle's position that man's natural habitat is the society of other men and that human development seems intended by nature to take place in the social context, Hackett suggests that a properly functioning military may be an ideal societal form.

> Living in a group demands some subordination of the self to the interests of the group. The military contract demands the total and almost unconditional subordination of the interests of the individual if the interests of the group should require it. This can lead to the surrender of life itself. It not infrequently does. Thus in an important respect the military would appear to be one of the more advanced forms of social institution.[8]

The Aristotelian notion of man as *zoon politicus* is worth some attention if only to contrast with the view of Hobbes mentioned earlier. Aristotle, and the classical Greeks generally, would not grant Hobbes's view that man's nature is totally egoistic, requiring political arrangements and constraining moral rules to be artificially imposed. The family and the state are in fact viewed as natural to man who works out his development in the context of these organizations: They are not essentially contrived to hold back man's selfish egoism but rather provide the context and education for each person's growth and contribution to the polis. In this view, political structures are intended to educate individuals for their contributive roles in human societies. Based on the fundamental and unique role of reason in the life of man, the Greek view seeks rational harmony within the individual and in the state; peace and not war would better describe the "natural" state of man. Balance, moderation, development of the intellect—these are the ethical aims appropriate to man and required to be fostered by the state. An ethic based on self-interest, cost-benefit, or the bottom-line must be totally uncongenial to this perspective of the role of man in society.

It may be necessary to distinguish between self-interest viewed as "selfishness" and self-interest viewed as "self-development." We attribute selfishness to those who seek their own advantage without regard to the consequences of their actions for others or in spite of causing harm to others. To develop one's talents can be viewed as self-interested action, but it need not be selfish. Certainly, some self-interested actions can be morally right and justifiably encouraged (developing one's mind or skills which will be employed for the benefit of all). It is the extreme egoistic sense of self-interested action (selfishness) which gives rise to Hobbesian views of the need for a governmental leviathan. It is also selfishness which characterizes the careerist and his organizational counterpart, militarism.

The root notion of service to the polity seems more accurate and appropriate for understanding the military profession than does the root notion of social contract. William May suggested the possibility that social contract theories remove individuals from active participation in the governing process. "Government is not what one does but what one purchases with taxes." Citizens may, in this view, be active at the founding and dissolution of the state but passive in between. One can easily venture a parallel suggestion when the military function is also viewed as a contractual relationship with the society: "Defense is not what one does but what one purchases with taxes." Thus the average citizen, especially when not under immediate threat of attack, may not feel any obligation to provide anything other than financial support to the military profession; his role is passive. Even when the nation is under immediate attack, if the military function is viewed as contractual only, the nonmilitary citizen remains passive and expects the military professional to protect his client (society) against external enemies.

May had suggested that the extended application of the social contract thesis to the profession in general produces "adversarial" relationships; society as the client of the professions and faced with the threat of the negative (pain, lawsuits, crime, aggression, and the like) is involved only in the formation and dissolution of the relationship which has the professional protecting the client against threats. Analogies in medicine and law are obvious, but perhaps the critical notion to be learned from May is that when governments or professions are dominated by negative motives (formed to suppress evil) rather than positive motives (formed to promote the general good), adversarial relationships are almost certain to be promoted. It is easy to agree with his concern that when professional authority is invoked by fear, it will be difficult to limit and will ultimately generate resentment against the professionals.

Jacques Barzun observed that for the past decade, the professions have been under fire because the competence and ethical standards displayed by many practitioners in medicine, law, education, and other professions have been exposed and found wanting.

> The message for the professions today is that their one hope of survival with anything like their present freedom is the recovery of mental and moral force. No profession can live and flourish on just one of the two. For its "practical purpose" it requires the best knowledge and its effective use. But since that purpose is to transfer the good of that knowledge from the possessor to another person, the moral element necessarily comes into play. *Moral* here does not mean merely honest; it refers to the nature of any encounter between two human beings.[9]

Like the professions for which Barzun has expressed concern, the military profession has also been "under siege" and needs to reexamine, if not to recover, its "mental and moral force." These reflections contrasting the egoistic foundations of social contract theories with classical Greek notions of man may lead us to fruitful judgments concerning the ethical dimensions of military leadership.

Ethical Implications

The military leader who views his oath of office as merely a contractual arrangement with his government sets the stage for a style of leadership critically different from the leader who views that oath as his pledge to contribute to the common good of his society. For the former, "duty, honor, country" is a slogan adopted temporarily until the contract is completed; for the latter, "duty, honor, country" is a way of life adopted for the good of all and accepted as a moral commitment not subject to contractual negotiations.

If one adopts the contractual view, it is relatively easy to attempt to divorce the military function from moral considerations. War is a dirty business, and the task facing this military leader is to develop armies and weapons systems which can efficiently destroy potential enemies; the body count is the bottom line. This conception is analogous to the adoption of the contractual view in the teaching profession, which envisions the role of the teacher as transmitter of value-free objective knowledge, packaged and distributed; grade-point average is the bottom line. Neither approach accepts responsibility for forming the character of the people being led (to war or to knowledge), and hence there is no predicting the uses to which their weapons or knowledge may be directed. But leadership is not a value-free enterprise; approaches which ignore the critical ethical dimensions of leadership must always be viewed as unsatisfactory. This latter assertion assumes, of course, that the role of the professions, and especially the military profession, is best viewed as more nearly approximating the Aristotelian than the Hobbesian idea.

In the American context, a leadership committed to the development of character can be on precarious ground. In our pluralistic society, there will always be the question, what kind of character, what virtues can be legitimately taught and inculcated? It seems clear, however, that an ethic for any of the public professions based on a total laissez faire, egoistic, and self-interested view of man will not do. Professions which do not exercise constraints over their members' standards of competence and over the costs of professional services invite governmental controls. Professions whose members lose sight of their service function in society and allow the values of the marketplace to become dominant invite unionization. Precarious ground or not, concern for virtue among professionals is critical if the professions are going to survive with anything at all like their past and current status. The medical, legal, and military functions continue to be critical to society, but that is not to be confused with continuing preeminence of the associated professionals.

> What every professional should bear in mind is the distinction between a profession and a function. The function may well be eternal; but the profession, which is the cluster of practices and relationships arising from the function at a given time and place, can be destroyed—or can destroy itself-very rapidly.[10]

The function of the military profession (its mission) is relatively well fixed; and it is a noble one whether it is characterized as the management of violence (Huntington), the containment of violence (Hackett), or as constabulary (Janowitz). The latter two characterizations are similar and seem most accurate for the U.S. military profession currently. They do not presume so wide a gulf between war and peace as has been the American predilection prior to the end of World War II, nor do they avoid the essential moral concern that total war, with its potential for the destruction of all humanity, has become an irrational option. Already one sees that the military leader cannot afford the luxury, if luxury is what it is, of viewing his function in some sort of "scientific" or objective value-free way. The uses of military force always involve moral considerations; the decision to go to war is a moral decision; and the judgments on the employment of means are always more than merely military judgments. At least since President Lincoln's acceptance of Lieber's "Instructions for the Government of Armies of the United States in the Field" in 1863, the public position of the United States has been that all is *not* fair in war. This position has been reaffirmed many times through the Hague and Geneva Conventions; in the Army pamphlet, *The Law of Land Warfare*; and through our participation in war crimes tribunals at Nuremberg and Tokyo after World War II. Military leaders are charged with the responsibility of observing the moral positions developed through this tradition, and with educating all members of the profession with regard to the provisions of these "laws of war."

The "military" virtues are virtues in any human society, pluralistic or not; but they are called military virtues because of their essential connection to the specific military function. The end (military mission) is essentially fixed—the choice of means to bring about that end often involves moral considerations and always requires a display of certain virtues in effecting those means. In some professions the most obvious specific virtues are easy to identify; in medicine and law, for example, client confidentiality receives unanimous, clear, dominant, and obvious emphasis. The military virtues are no less obvious: *subordination of the good of the self to the good of the nation and military unit, courage, obedience, loyalty, integrity.* I have argued elsewhere[11] that integrity is the foundation virtue for military leaders if they wish to successfully develop loyalty and obedience in their subordinates. But the critical thing to notice here is that these virtues are obvious because of their functional necessity; success in battle is impossible without them; preparation for battle requires their inculcation. Please note that these moral virtues are not merely "nice to have," they are functional imperatives in the military profession. Notice also that if the list is a correct one and self-subordination is as crucial as I believe it to be to the military function, then a contractual view of one's role in the profession generated from the Hobbesian view of man cannot adequately serve as the ethical foundation for military leadership.

Superior-Subordinate Relationships

Given the enormous authority over the lives of subordinates that the hierarchical military structure provides to its leaders, what are the moral demands on those to whom subordinates are required to be loyal and obedient? Again the fundamental position on the nature of human relationships is extremely relevant. If the relationship between superior and subordinate is viewed as merely contractual, then each association takes on the dimensions of a transaction.[12] The subordinate expects that the superior will respond to his needs; the superior expects that subordinates will "do their job" in response to his commands. Each has contracted to act in specified fashion. The more Aristotelian view of leadership would have the leader accept responsibility for transforming subordinates with an eye to inculcating the virtues mentioned earlier. The transactional leader places emphasis on objective performance; the transformational leader adds to performance an emphasis on education. The transactional leader is less likely to accept responsibility when his mission fails; in those cases he can easily place the blame on subordinates who did not "fulfill their contract." The transformational leader resembles more the "good leader" depicted by Lao Tzu in the quotation appearing at the beginning of this chapter. The contrast between these two approaches seems authentic when placed in practical context as in the following comments made by officers participating in the Army War College's study of professionalism:

> [There is] fear in the subordinate of relief and a bad Officer Effectiveness Report if he admits that his unit is less than perfect or he is presenting a point his superior doesn't want to hear. . . . The subordinate must have the integrity to "tell it like it is" in spite of fear for his career, etc., while the superior owes it to his subordinate to help him as much as possible as opposed to the attitude of "you get it squared away or I'll get someone who will" over a one-time deficiency.
>
> Across the board the Officer Corps is lacking in their responsibilities of looking out for the welfare of subordinates. Everyone is afraid to make a mistake with someone always looking over his shoulder.
>
> They are afraid that if they delegate authority to subordinates . . . they themselves will suffer. . . . Subordinates are not being properly developed and there is a general feeling among junior officers that seniors are untouchable, unapproachable, unreasonable, and constantly looking for mistakes. . . . A commander who takes a genuine interest in the welfare and training of his subordinates is getting rarer.[13]

It is easy to see from these comments made by officers of different ranks that their perceptions of actual leadership practice in 1970 was that it was transactional (in our terms) when it ought to have been transformational. Is it going too far to attribute many of the moral lapses in the military profession in the United States in recent years to the contractual (transactional) relationship? One of the ethical scandals accompanying the all-volunteer army conception in the middle and late 1970s was the occurrence of recruiting irregularities. Several newspaper articles reported on congressional investigations which revealed that fictitious names were placed on computers to meet recruiting quotas; police records were altered so that those possessing them could be fraudulently enlisted; test scores were altered so that others could be qualified for enlistment. The enlistment quota was viewed by many as a contract, a "bottom line"; and the resulting pressures were seen by some recruiters as reason enough to cheat and lie. Similar pressures, sometimes generated by unrealistic goals or demands for perfection, are frequently adduced as reasons for false reporting of AWOL rates, false readiness reports, cheating on training examinations, false aircraft incommission reports, and falsification of a host of other quantitative indicators which we have institutionalized and used to evaluate the effectiveness of our leaders at all levels.

Common sense suggests that the bottom-line ethic most easily accompanies institutionalized overemphasis on quantitative measurements of leadership. "When we can't measure the things that are important, we ascribe importance to the things we can measure" (attributed, perhaps erroneously, to Milton). Along with the emphasis on quantitative measurements comes often the requirement to report 100 percent of the quantity measured. Misinterpretation of a "zero-defects" program can lead and has led subordinates to believe that a single mistake or any performance that produces a "bottom line" that is less than 100 percent can lead to career disaster. Professor Flammer suggested that the institutional pressures generated by exaggerated emphasis on "zero-defects" led to bad superior-subordinate relationships, even to the point of compromised integrity:

> (The Zero Defects System), interpreted literally, as some image-conscious and ambitious commanders were inclined to do, automatically moved from the realm of the plausible and desirable to the impossible and impractical. In many instances, the program evolved into a "Zero Error Mentality," that is, the commander felt that his command had to be error free. . . . Yet outlawing risk precludes initiative, which is a basic requisite for modern combat effectiveness. In the end, many errors were made and consequently covered up, for the zero error mentality is automatically wedded to the grotesque philosophy that it is worse to report a mistake than it is to make one. [14]

The transformational leader sets the moral tone for his subordinates by the example of integrity he provides in both his official duties and in his private life. Honesty cannot be instilled by contract—but it may be enhanced by education about its importance to mission accomplishment and by example. Courage cannot be instilled by contractual arrangement, nor should it be expected if the basic mission orientation is merely contractual. It seems clear that selfishness is more generated than sublimated by any contractual/ transactional grounding of the military ethic. Army Chief of Staff General Edward C. Meyer seemed to be summarizing this point of view when he commented recently: "The obligation of service and commitment inherent in the military ethic imposes burdens not customary in the larger society where obligations are normally contractual in nature and limited in degree of personal sacrifice expected. For the soldier, the obligation is complete: to death if necessary."[15]

Is Professional Competence a Moral Obligation?

It is not immoral under normal circumstances to fail a course in school. If a military person is incapable of learning to deal appropriately with a sophisticated weapons system, that is not immoral. But the leader who knowingly assigns the incapable to equipment they cannot operate is not merely foolish; where the stakes are so high in terms of the survival of his society, loss of human life, and use of national treasure, it seems clear he has entered the moral realm. With respect to the development of tactics, weaponry, long-range strategy, and the conditions for employing those weapons systems which pose serious threats to noncombatants, the military leader's competence is a crucial issue. Literally, he has a moral obligation to be competent in these areas. There are analogies in other professions. Judges are morally obliged to research and understand legal precedent relevant to cases over which they have jurisdiction. Incompetence on the judge's part can lead to injustice; and, of course, justice is a very important moral value. Surgeons are morally obliged to develop an understanding of the human organs on which they operate, and they are obliged to study and understand surgical techniques before deciding to employ them. In these areas it seems clear that the obligation to be competent is not merely prudent; where justice and human life are at stake, and where authority to act has been bestowed, the obligation to be competent must be viewed as a moral one. Often in the military context, the authority of the military leader to act is nearly absolute and the stakes at issue are crucial to society. The strength of the moral obligation must be commensurate with that responsibility.

Within the context of the professional ethic, it appears the line between incompetence and immorality is a very thin line, perhaps most obviously so in the military profession. It is obvious that an incompetent physician may, in a lifetime of practicing bad medicine, harm many of his patients, perhaps even cause some deaths. It is also disheartening to contemplate the damage that an incompetent junior high school teacher may do to developing young minds. But the incompetent military leader may bring about needless loss of life and indeed, at the extreme, may have at his fingertips, the ability to destroy humanity as we know it. Given this critical uniqueness of the role of military leaders, no nation can afford to have them be intellectually incompetent or morally insensitive. Further, it seems clear that military leaders must extend this concern for competence to all levels of the military hierarchy. It is also quite clear that neither competence nor moral sensitivity are acquired by mere contract; military leadership in these areas must proceed by example and by education. Transformational leadership holds far more promise than transactional leadership where competence and character are at issue.

Perhaps we may lay at the door of advancing technology some of the explanation for our need to connect moral concerns with military leadership in a fashion that was unnecessary for professionals of the past. When there was some possibility that the majority of persons wearing uniforms were likely to confront an enemy in direct combat, the primacy of courage was so obvious as not to require commentary. When unit survival in battle depended on each soldier's fulfilling his assigned task, the need for subordination of self to the common good, conceptions of loyalty and obedience were all so clearly seen as fundamental and functionally imperative that example and encouragement were adequate to guarantee their inculcation. But in the modern U.S. military services, there is great need to call attention to the ultimate purpose of the military profession because technological specialization has brought about a state of affairs that places the majority of uniform wearers in specialized roles remote from anything resembling battle engagements in past wars. Even those in direct control of our most devastating weapons systems will never confront their enemies face-to-face; indeed, their knowledge of the target of their weapons is frequently restricted to location and numbers

As early as 1960, Professor Janowitz was pointing out that the tasks of military leadership had become segmented into at least three identifiable characterizations: the direct combat roles of the heroic leader, the organizational and administrative functions of the military manager, and the specialized skills of the military technologist.[16] The traditional military virtues and moral considerations are most easily associated with the heroic leader because he most directly employs the instruments of violence and places himself and his men at risk. The moral consequences of incompetence in that role are easiest to discern. Not so with the leader whose essential contribution to the profession is the management of large contracts, or developmental programs, or large numbers of people engaged in support functions. He may see himself in a role analogous to that of a manager in a large business firm or industrial complex and may use analogous measures of successful operation: productivity, cost effectiveness, bottom-line numbers. In this environment it is remarkably easy to lose sight of the ultimate function of the military profession. What kinds of measurements are the relevant ones to determine if the profession is best prepared to defend our way of life? Productivity is important only if the "product" is contributing to the success of the military function. In a psychological warfare campaign, for example, does the number of sorties flown and the number of leaflets dropped (easily measured and easily increased) provide a measure of the success of the psychological operation?

The military technologist may be the farthest removed from the direct military function. He may spend an entire career in military laboratories, contributing to basic research in optical physics, laser development, analysis of radiation effects, development of computer software, and so on. He may be outnumbered by the civilian researchers participating in the same projects, working the same hours, and differing only in the circumstances of pay and work uniform. How much more like the civilian specialist his daily life appears to be than like the traditional military leader whose principal concerns might have been the inculcation in his subordinates of unity, loyalty, obedience, and the other military virtues. The officer researcher's status in the military profession seems more to resemble that of the military doctor than that of the traditional heroic leader. The military doctor may identify more closely with the medical profession than with the military profession. But both the military technologist and the military doctor may be called upon to place themselves at risk by carrying out their specialized functions in combat zones, while their civilian colleagues are not bound by the same unlimited liability. The danger of diminishing effectiveness of the military profession seems directly proportional to the growing identification of military specialists (technologists or managers) with their specialty at the cost of less identification with the profession of arms.

It is important to notice that often the rewards of daily effort are connected immediately with one's specialized activity and only mediately with the ultimate military function. This is not often true in other professions. The medical doctor who saves a life by timely surgery or relieves pain by curing an illness sees himself fulfilling his function directly and daily. The air force major who solves a critical data systems problem leading to more efficient usage of the comptroller's computers gets the immediate fulfillment of the data systems analyst but may have to extrapolate remarkably well to perceive herself as contributing to the ultimate military mission. The moral dimensions of competence in this environment are easily overlooked, perhaps replaced entirely by prudential considerations. Duty, honor, country; responsibility for the lives of one's subordinates; victory on the battlefield—all seem remote from the many specialized tasks performed in the extremely complex, technologically oriented, modern military structure.

As the distinction between certain military and civilian "jobs" becomes narrower, the relationship between leader and led may have a tendency to become even more contractual and less transformational. It is not sheer coincidence that the standard terminology for civilian assistance to the military has included the phrase "defense contractor." With the word "contract" comes the emphasis on the values of the marketplace, concern for working hours, pay scales, and perhaps even collective bargaining. Charles Moskos has highlighted perceivable dangers to military effectiveness and legitimacy should the military institution see its traditional professional values replaced by the self-interested values of the contractors who work so closely with the military."[17]

Conclusions

The nature of modern defense policy and the composition of the U.S. defense organization have placed strains on the professional military ethic. Complexity, however much it may conceal the functional importance of the ethical-military virtues, is not an excuse for failure to understand the crucial role these virtues must play. With complicated command, control, and communications networks comes an even more critical need for integrity in reporting. Command decisions are more centralized but depend entirely on honest inputs. There is still need for the heroic leader, but his role must be complemented by the military manager and the military technologist. It is not inconceivable that our most able military professionals will have to demonstrate characteristics of all these roles, sometimes all at the same time.

In an era when miscalculation can lead to tragic consequences for humanity, technological competence takes on an added and crucial moral dimension. If, under the umbrella of a nuclear deterrent posture, future military engagements must be carried out with the intention of containing violence at the lowest possible level, military leaders will have to be totally aware of the political uses of the military instrument. In the context of limited engagements for specific political aims, courageous action and the subordination of self to mission accomplishment become more difficult for the military professional (especially for those immersed in the ethos of "total victory"), but even more important than ever before. Integrity, obedience, loyalty—these qualities take on even more significance in the modern military as it becomes more difficult for military leaders to inculcate them in their people. The military function retains its noble and necessary role of protection of a way of life; the military profession in the United States will be equal to the task of carrying out that function only in proportion to its ability to attract and retain leaders who understand the ethical dimensions of professional competence and who themselves exemplify the highest intellectual and moral qualities.

Notes

1. In July 1980, William May (currently at the Kennedy Center for the Study of Ethics, Georgetown University) read a paper on "Adversarialism in America" at Vassar College as part of a workshop on professional ethics sponsored by The Hastings Center. His paper has caused me to reevaluate formerly held views of social-contract theories, but Professor May should not be held responsible for any distortions of his insights at my hands.

2.These two views are not proposed as the *only* approaches to citizen-state relationships or to leadership-follower relationships. I deal only with these two in this chapter because (1) it seems likely that social-contract theory approaches are most common, and (2) I think they easily lead to harmful practices and should be supplanted by an approach based on the classical conception of the polity.

3. U.S. Army War College, *Study on Military Professionalism* (Carlisle Barracks, Pa., 1970), B-1-2.

4. Max Lerner, "The Shame of the Professions," *Saturday Review 3,* 1975, 11.

5. Samuel P. Huntington, *The Soldier and the State* (New York: Random House, 1957), ch. 3.

6. Alfred Vagts, *A History of Militarism* (New York, Macmillan, 1959).

7. Lieutenant General Sir John W. Hackett, *The Profession of Arms* (London: Times Publishing, 1962).

8. Hackett, *The Profession of Arms*, 45.

9. Jacques Barzun, "The Professions Under Siege," *Harper's* 257 (1541), 1978, 68.

10. Barzun, "Under Siege," 63.

11. "*The Ethics of Leadership I.*"

12. The terms "transactional leadership" and "transformational leadership" are borrowed from William May (Note 1), who in turn credits their usage to James McGregor Burns.

13. *Study on Military Professionalism*, 14-16.

14. Philip M. Flammer, "Conflicting Loyalties and the American Military Ethic," *American Behavioral Scientist* (May/June 1976), 597.

15. General Edward C. Meyer, "Professional Ethics Is Key to Well-Led, Trained Army," *Army* 30 (1980), 14.

16. Morris Janowitz, *The Professional Soldier* (New York: Macmillan, 1960), ch. 2.

17. Charles C. Moskos Jr., "From Institution to Occupation," *Armed Forces and Society* 4 (1977), 41-50.

Chapter 9

THE MILITARY: A NOBLE PROFESSION

For me, as for many young men (our traditional citizen-soldiers), military experience was just a vivid stopping place on the road to a more fruitful vocation. But the opportunity to teach philosophy at the United States Air Force Academy brought with it the challenge to examine the military profession more seriously. Philosophy colleagues have said that a military mind is not openly free for the study of philosophy. Some military colleagues agree with the philosophers—military men who think too much become Hamlets; they will not be effective decision-makers. Herein lies the challenge. Who can embrace a profession, dedicate a lifetime to a line of work in which one's very rationality would appear to be a detriment? Can the military life possibly provide a noble profession for man?

While it seems obvious that our reasons for remaining in a given profession for a lifetime may often differ from our initial reasons for entering that profession, it is nevertheless instructive to ask what the criteria are for judging professions. What are the prestige professions in our society? Why are some esteemed more than others? Ask any group of young people these questions, as I have done often, and the answers come very quickly. Medicine, law, the ministry, science, politics (sometimes), teaching (occasionally)—these are readily identified. After the superficial suggestions that we admire these professions, especially medicine and law, because of the high income of doctors, lawyers, and judges, more serious probings follow. Isn't it true that we admire the medical profession because when we view the doctor as doctor, not as wage earner, we note that his function concerns a very high human value—life itself? It is because we view life to be so precious that we can so readily agree that the profession whose principal function is to preserve life deserves our approbation. It is not merely bare existence the doctor helps us with; it is the quality of life that also concerns us. We value highly a life characterized by good health as distinguished from daily physical misery, mental disorder, etc. Analogously, the high human value which serves as the functional objective for the profession of law is justice. We value justice for it also impacts on the quality of human life as we envision its possibilities for every member of our society. The legal profession should make it possible for each man to lead a just life. Life and justice—two noble ends for professions to pursue.

Reprinted with permission from *Notre Dame Magazine*, February 1974, 14-18.

If we wish to ask whether the military profession deserves our esteem also, then we must inquire about its essential function. As I conceive it, the military, too, is concerned about the quality of life. The most crucial function of the military in a free nation is to preserve that nation's way of life. For some, surely the way in which we lead our lives may be even more important than life itself. Plato has Socrates suggesting in the *Apology* that the good man, the wise man, concerns himself far more with whether he does right or wrong than with whether he lives or dies. If our way of life is a very high human value, then the profession whose primary function is to preserve that way of life must be as deserving of our esteem as other noble professions which have primary concern for the quality of life. The soldier's function is particularly crucial in the light of our previous observations about medicine and law, for it would seem to provide the very conditions which make the practice of other professions possible. The man who wears his country's uniform need not, on this consideration, move to the back of the bus. This assumes, of course, that the way of life is worth preserving. We feel justified in that assumption for our own society; clearly it would make sense in some societies, in some historical periods, to question critically that assumption.

What, then, can we objectively report about the present status and future prospects of the profession of arms in the United States? Obviously, given the current temper of a society relieved to be extricated from overt involvement in Vietnam, relieved additionally at the relaxation of tensions with the Soviet Union and China, the American professional military can expect to prepare for its job with far less of the national resources (men and money) than it has had available to it for the past several years. Further, with the passing of the era of universal military conscription, we may well experience some difference in the reasons men have for entering the military services. Already it is evident that the number of young men seeking ROTC appointments has diminished considerably on most of our college campuses. This may be all to the good for the military, oddly enough, for it is very possible that many of those who seek out ROTC without the pressure of the draft have seriously considered full-time military careers. The size of our military forces will probably not become inordinately small for a number of obvious reasons. The great fear of the bomb that all of us have lived under for a number of years seems to have dissipated itself recently in American society. Perhaps this is because of confidence in a strategy of deterrence (our ability to retaliate is so strong that no one will dare launch a nuclear attack); perhaps one can only view a crisis as real for a limited amount of time if it does not materialize and continues to remain in the background. Whatever the causes which incline us toward military reductions, there remains some minimum level of possible response to any military threat below which neither our civilian nor military leaders dare go. In the opinion of most informed observers, this minimum level of response demands the continued existence of larger force structures than our country has been accustomed to during the postwar periods prior to 1945.

Even given the compelling aim of nuclear survival, however, the military action in Korea, in Southeast Asia, in the Middle East, and in India and Pakistan have all served as evidence that American military forces can expect to be employed in political roles far short of fighting for our immediate national survival. These uses of our forces, apart from the ongoing national strategy of nuclear deterrence, have provided us with a number of moral problems about which, as a nation, we have disagreed and have become extremely troubled. Many observers of American attitudes toward war have pointed out that in many of our past wars we have been crusaders who fought to "make the world safe for democracy" or to defend ourselves from treacherous aggression. The final goal of such wars has generally been conceived as "total victory" or "unconditional surrender" of the enemy. We have rarely followed the Clausewitzian notion of using our war-making capability as one of many instruments of our international political policies. Recent involvement in limited wars suggests that our national policy, if not our national sentiment, has shifted. Several of our recent presidents have commented on the problems of maintaining both a deterrent posture and a combat-ready force for limited wars. Perhaps our previous tradition of fighting wars whose goal was total victory over the enemy has contributed to the confusion surrounding both the Korean and Vietnam involvements.

Given this complex state of affairs, how may those officers who comprise the leadership corps of the military view their role in the profession? Must they become experts in world politics as well as super technicians who are capable of directing the sophisticated weapons systems of a computerized world? The answer to the latter question is clearly yes. We need officers today who understand the complexities of international politics because some uniformed persons will be making recommendations to our highest civilian policy makers. We need highly educated econometricians who can plan for and guide sophisticated logistical systems. We need experts in procurement and in contracting and in management who can overcome some of our past ineptitudes in weapons acquisitions. We need computer experts and personnel officers, aircraft commanders and ship commanders, nuclear experts and electronic geniuses—all these men must be wearing uniforms. We need decision makers who are both intellectually competent and morally sensitive. It is simply false that this nation or the human world as we know it can survive if the men who hold our highest military positions are really characterized by our stereotyped image of the military mind.

That the image persists is readily apparent. Note the contrast in two popular television series today. In *Marcus Welby, M.D.*, we see the gracious portrayal of the family physician, totally dedicated to serving the people in his community. Dr. Welby is competent, kind, always morally as well as medically concerned for the welfare of his patients. Consider at the same time the manner in which high-ranking officers are portrayed in the series *M.A.S.H.* The message there is an old one and a clear one: Intellect and competence are inversely proportional to rank and length of service. High-ranking officers are, in fact, portrayed as bumbling idiots.

Tragic! Both that this image persists and that there are occasional members of the uniformed services who have exhibited some characteristics of the stereotype. Speaking for those officers whose careers I have followed most closely, graduates of the Air Force Academy, I can factually verify that there are great young men moving into positions of authority. The level of education among career officers is rising. Among those of our graduates who have reached the ten-year point in their careers, approximately 60 percent have earned master's degrees or higher. Leadership in all of the military services is less authoritarian than ever before in history. Rational persuasion is becoming the rule rather than the exception. In contemporary society, that becomes increasingly critical. The military no less than the school, the street, and the Church is learning that authority by itself no longer commands the obedience of the young and the subordinate. Great emphasis is being placed on guaranteeing equal opportunities for all minority groups and women. Young officers with bright ideas are being heard—but the young are short on patience. Older officers with experienced patriotism are concerned that values for which their men have died may be set aside. Both concerns are understandable; and with improved communications, both will be ameliorated.

The profession of arms persists. The existence of world-destroying weapons systems argues for higher standards for the men who pursue this calling than ever before. If we have military leaders who are not our best thinkers, then they must be replaced by men of vision and moral understanding. But this will happen only if those young men with the requisite abilities see the challenge and pursue the profession of arms. I am convinced that human survival is possible only if *good* men (intellectually and morally good men) hold the reins of military leadership. Those who have the ability but become discouraged because progress through the bureaucracy is slow leave the reins of leadership to the mediocre. In some professions this is easily remedied. The inept doctor will be found out before too much damage is done, the incompetent or unscrupulous lawyer may be disbarred. But the military professional who is not equal to the responsibilities we ask of him today could trigger the destruction of mankind.

The military profession today is still a demanding one. It requires more technical ability than ever before. It is using streamlined techniques of management but needs to continue seeking ways to do more with less. In addition to the high premium being placed on more intellectual sophistication in the scientific, political, economic and managerial spheres, it must place added emphasis on the increasingly complex moral sphere. The profession of arms has always valued courage, personal and group loyalty, self-sacrifice, self-discipline, and integrity. Recent events have highlighted the need to reemphasize these values in the military and in many other areas of public service as well. Indeed, the reemphasis on these moral values in the profession of arms may well have a salutary effect on the society as a whole which frequently, and indeed recently, has exhibited a need for moral reexamination. Sir John Winthrop Hackett in the 1970 Harmon Memorial Lecture at the Air Force Academy provides us with a summary thought on the role of moral values in the military:

> A man can be selfish, cowardly, disloyal, false, fleeting, perjured and morally corrupt in a wide variety of other ways and still be outstandingly good in pursuits in which other imperatives bear than those upon the fighting man. He can be a superb *creative* artist, for example, or a scientist in the very top flight and still be a very bad man. What the bad man cannot be is a good sailor, or soldier, or airman. Military institutions thus form a repository of moral resource which should always be a source of strength within the state.

Chapter 10

WANTED: MORAL VIRTUES IN THE MILITARY

The "My Lai Massacre," a chillingly alliterative headline, quickly attracted and then retained public attention as the details emerged. Some refused to believe that young American soldiers could have killed unarmed prisoners, many of them obviously noncombatants, in large numbers. (According to the official report by Lieutenant General Peers, at least 175 were killed and the dead may have numbered more than 400.)

Some refused to believe that American officers could have given such orders in direct violation of our own laws, international agreements, and the obvious moral prohibitions against such killings, even in war. Some refused to believe that officers and noncommissioned officers could have been present at My Lai and participated in the killing of noncombatants. Some refused to believe that officers in each succeeding rank from lieutenant on up to major general in the division's chain of command had some knowledge of the events at My Lai and failed to investigate thoroughly, failed to report the events as required by regulation to higher headquarters, and may have participated in some fashion in covering up the details. But all these things happened.

This Vietnam war episode, which occurred in March 1968, raises a host of moral issues, many unique to the military profession, but all of continuing importance for professional military ethics. On the most generous accounts, the orders given by Lieutenant William Calley to his platoon were ambiguous on whether all inhabitants of My Lai were to be killed. If the order was clearly to kill without discriminating between combatant and noncombatant, then it was both immoral and illegal. If it was ambiguous, then it ought not to have been; where innocent life is at risk, combat leaders are morally obliged to train and control their men within the restraints so clearly delineated in the *Law of Land Warfare* (Army Field Manual 27-10). But whether the orders were illegitimate or ambiguous, once they had been given, the responsibilities of subordinates for their actions in responding to such orders involved serious moral questions.

The U.S. position on the commission of war crimes under orders was clearly stated in the *Law of Land Warfare* and emphatically asserted during the Nuremberg trials at the close of the Second World War. Subordinates who commit crimes at the order of a superior remain responsible for their actions if

Reprinted with permission from the *Hastings Center Report*, October 1985.

they knew or could reasonably be assumed to have known that the orders were unlawful. A reasonable person, even in the heat of combat, could hardly fail to see that killing unarmed prisoners, many of them women and children (even babies), was unlawful (and immoral). Indeed, some soldiers questioned the orders of Lieutenant Calley at the time, and some tried unsuccessfully to stop the killing.

Because many human lives and the success of military operations are frequently at stake, obedience to orders in the military hierarchy is a compelling obligation. Disobedience rightfully entails serious penalties. But in some contexts the obligation to avoid doing evil overrides the obligation to obey, and My Lai seems clearly to have been one of those occasions. But—who decides? The answer to this agonizing question is an easy one and an ancient one. Persons of good moral character make the right moral choices even when doing right can carry severe personal consequences. Good legal rules or good moral rules were not lacking; the rules were available and known but there were not enough men of good moral character to act rightly themselves and control the evil actions of others.

Parallels to the obedience issue exist in other professions. Nurses sometimes have moral difficulties with orders from doctors, which they perceive to go against the interests of their patients. The medical-moral conflict is analogous to the legitimacy-of-orders question raised above, but the consequences in the military case are often more extensive since many more lives and the policies governing an entire campaign may be at stake. But My Lai raises additional moral concerns. Putting aside personal considerations—fear of the unfamiliar, fear of death, and the spirit of angry revenge for the recent land mine deaths of fellow soldiers—did institutional policies contribute to the moral blindness of some soldiers at My Lai? How was success in battle generally measured in a "war of attrition"?

False Reporting and Cover-Ups

One way of measuring a unit's effectiveness in battle in Vietnam was the "body count." How many of the enemy were killed? On a clearly defined battlefield, with opposing sides wearing easily identifiable uniforms, the relative losses of fighting men on each side would be relevant information along with whether or not one side surrendered, ran away, and so on. But in a guerrilla war, where many of the enemy were not in uniform, and where they regularly hid among the rest of the population, counting every dead Vietnamese as a part of the enemy body count was misleading.

Some on our side treated the body count like the "bottom line" on a business ledger. This approach to measuring unit effectiveness may have been well intentioned since body count was, after all, an "objective" measure. But pressures to increase the body count and hence "look good" may have influenced the fearful and enhanced the careers of the ambitious. Who is responsible for evaluating institutional policies for their moral implications? Who deals with the subtle pressures to overlook moral means in search of favorable bottom lines?

The desire to look good and advance rapidly is not unique to the military profession; we find it in all large bureaucratic structures whether they are business firms, government agencies, or educational institutions. These concerns often encourage false reporting (in order to appear error free) or concealing problems in order to avoid the appearance of incompetence. When a senior person gets away with such deceptions and moves rapidly up the promotion ladder the morale of organization members suffers seriously and we find widespread cynicism regarding the fairness of our promotion systems. Within the military structure false reporting and cover-ups are more serious than in many other professions because of the trust we place in our military leaders and because human life so frequently rests on decisions based on what may be false information.

Though upstaged soon afterwards by Watergate, the cover-up of the My Lai affair prior to the thorough investigation conducted by Lieutenant General Peers and his committee is a classic case of abjuring responsibility for the acts of subordinates. The two cover-ups seem analogous, but the deaths that occurred at My Lai make that episode more grievous.

The military profession must continue to stress individual moral responsibility for the actions of its members but must also be concerned about the moral responsibilities of leaders at every level of command. General Yamashita of Japan was executed after World War II on the grounds that as commander he was responsible for the atrocities committed by his men in the Philippines even though he did not order the atrocities nor was he physically present to halt them when they occurred. Commanders are responsible for tactics employed in war, and for insisting that the laws of war, and training in those laws, be observed. How can we assure that both our military leaders and their subordinates will accept their moral responsibilities in conjunction with their fighting responsibilities?

Beyond Moral Codes

Many professions have promulgated codes of ethics, which specify standards of performance and conduct for their members. The military too has its ethical codes, written and unwritten, ideal and practical. But codes alone and knowledge of what is right have never been sufficient to guarantee right conduct. Doctors and defense attorneys schooled in the codes of ethics of their professions sometimes appear more interested in their fees than in the well-being of their patients and clients.

The careerist in the military profession (more interested in image and promotion than the military mission) is the analogue of the shyster. Recently, a government official suggested in more than jest that our military leaders are "more concerned about protecting their retirement benefits than they are about protecting the security of the American people." This comment obviously does great disservice to our many dedicated and honorable military leaders—but it highlights our concern that professionals not be distracted from their essential service to society.

Many on our side of the Vietnam War performed bravely and even nobly. Despite the attempts of his captors to break his resolve, Admiral Jim Stockdale insisted upon maintaining the military cohesion of our prisoners of war; he suffered torture for years and even disfigured himself to avoid being used for propaganda purposes. Air Force Captain Lance Sijan, seriously injured and unable to walk, would not allow a crew member from a rescue helicopter to descend a ladder to aid him because of the nearby enemy gunners. That act eventually cost the captain his life. He evaded capture for forty-six days, inching through jungle terrain on his back without food and water.

Courage, selflessness, loyalty—these are the qualities we seek in our military professionals, but knowing about them does not produce them in a crisis. It is moral character we seek, must have, at every level of military leadership. In this regard, the recent resurgence of virtue ethics in philosophy classrooms around the country has special significance for the military profession. Moral education is important, indeed crucial, but it must include an understanding of the need for developing the moral virtues in those who lead our professions. Only persons of habitual integrity and moral sensitivity can be trusted to take into account the rights of noncombatants, to perceive when orders are unlawful or immoral, to separate concern for image from concern for mission, to report honestly, to perceive when institutional policies unnecessarily strain the moral fiber of subordinates, and to serve society before self.

Only if we can select persons of excellent moral character to serve and lead the profession of arms can we hope that My Lai will remain an aberration and not a symbol of a society that has lost its moral compass.

Chapter 11

PROFESSIONAL INTEGRITY

Some years ago, one of the students in my medical ethics class approached me after the major research paper had been graded (it was worth 40 percent of the grade in the course). This student had worked hard during the course and had also worked hard on this twenty-page paper but it was clearly a solid B paper, and there was tragic disappointment on the face of this student. "I need an A on this paper to keep my A in the course," he said. "Please, you must raise my paper grade or you'll jeopardize my chance to be admitted to medical school."

Now I was very much interested in helping this student achieve admission to med school because I believed he had the potential to be an excellent physician, and I had said as much in the strong letter of reference I had written for him and sent to several med schools. But raise his grade on the basis of this request? My immediate response, provided almost automatically, was, "I *can't* do that."

In a very real sense, what I want to discuss with you tonight is bound up with that answer—"I can't do that." When I gave that answer, I didn't mean that I wasn't *able* to do that or that I didn't have the *authority* to do that. Physically and from the perspective of being the only instructor in the course, I *could* have raised that grade. And I didn't mean that fear of external consequences prevented me from changing that grade, i.e., fear that I might get caught and possibly lose my job. No, what I meant was, I can't change that grade because it would be wrong to do so for a number of good reasons. It would be *unfair* because the work really was not A work—it would be inappropriate to base student grades on "need to get into medical school" rather than "quality of work"—it would be unfair to other students whose work was graded on the basis of qualitative merit—all of these are certainly good reasons why "I can't do that." But perhaps what I also meant was that changing that grade to one I did not believe was earned would be a violation of my own integrity. My personal integrity, my self-respect, my ability to live with myself if I knowingly chose to do what I believed to be morally wrong was probably a good part of the meaning of the sentence "I can't do that."

But personal integrity is not the end of the story here. It seems to me there is also such a thing as *professional* integrity which is related to, perhaps dependent upon, certainly compatible with, but different from personal integrity.

This chapter was first presented as the Alice McDermott Memorial Lecture in Applied Ethics at the United States Air Force Academy on April 3, 1996. Versions of it have since appeared in a number of publications.

There are communal or corporate values associated with the teaching profession that place role-specific constraints on my behavior, and these are in addition to the normal moral values that I have as an ordinary moral agent. One thinks immediately of the special obligation to be competent in the subject matter and in teaching techniques. Proper preparation; special concern for each student's intellectual and, yes, character development; fair and timely evaluation of student work—all of these and more constitute special obligations of teaching professionals. And the teacher, who is literally "in front" of the students constantly must be totally conscious of the example which he or she sets for students—we teach by what we are and do, perhaps even more than by what we say. Maybe all of this was what was constraining me—maybe this is what I meant when I said, "I can't do that." I have special responsibilities to the institution, to my professional colleagues, and to the community I serve in this profession which really do matter to the well-being of our community, and they *trust* me.

Consider a more complicated case, this time from the medical profession. As a general practitioner, I've just received the results of the blood tests on my 23-year-old male patient and he is HIV positive. He is also engaged to be married. I point out to him his responsibility to inform his fiancée because she has a right to know about the danger to her and to any future children they might have. He reacts very emotionally to my suggestion because he believes she will refuse to marry him if she learns he has the AIDS virus. He says to me, "you must keep my condition a secret from her and from everyone. You're bound by the principle of patient confidentiality." Upon reflection, I reply, "*I can't do that.*"

Now, what I mean when I say "I can't do that" is that the moral principles that guide me as a medical professional require me to act but in this case their guidance is not unambiguous. The principle of respect for my patient's autonomy by observing confidentiality is a very important one, and it does indeed constrain my conduct. But the competing obligation I have to prevent harm is also very relevant in this case, and if I cannot persuade my patient to tell his fiancée himself, then I may judge that my duty to prevent harm overrides my duty to observe confidentiality in this case. My professional integrity is bound up in these competing moral principles and although it is extremely controversial here, I tell my patient, "I can't do that."

It's the spring of 1968, and I'm a young sergeant in a combat infantry company in South Vietnam. My platoon has captured an entire village of suspected Viet Cong sympathizers: 400 people, women, old people, children, and babies. We found no weapons in the village. My lieutenant orders us to herd them all over to the roadside ditch and shoot them. I say to him, "I can't do that." What I mean is, *we* can't do that—no one can do that. I know that I have a duty to obey the orders of my superiors, but I know that this order is in direct conflict with both my country's laws and with the fundamental moral law against harming the innocent. Several years earlier, in confirming the Yamashita death sentence, General MacArthur said: "The soldier, be he friend or foe, is charged with the protection of the weak and unarmed. It is the very essence and reason of his being. When he violates this sacred trust, he not only profanes his entire cult but threatens the fabric of international society." In this case of conflicting duties, my professional integrity tells me that my higher duty is to avoid harming the innocent, and when I'm ordered to kill babies—I can't do that.

These examples from education, medicine, and the military may help us to focus on this fuzzy notion of professional integrity. Integrity itself is a much-used term but very much in need of analysis. When we use the word "integrity" in a moral context we refer to the *whole* moral character of a person and we most frequently allude to one's personal integrity. When we say to someone, "don't compromise your integrity," we usually mean, "act in accordance with your moral principles within your value system. Be consistent." There is a real sense in which integrity encompasses our personal identity. As Polonius has it, "To thine ownself be true." But we must be very careful here. Consistency is not all there is to personal integrity. There is little merit in being consistent with your principles if "thine ownself" is egoistic, treacherous, criminal, and abusive. This is why integrity has to do with "wholeness," with one's entire character, and what that moral character is like is what counts. And subscribing to decent moral principles is not enough—we must *act* on decent principles—consistently. Others have noted accurately that integrity is the bridge between character and conduct.

Several centuries ago, Aristotle pointed out that moral credit is not automatic when right actions are done nor is it enough to know what is right or to say what is right. He suggested that we are morally praiseworthy when we do a right action if we, first of all, *know* that the action is right, secondly, *choose* the act for its own sake because we know it is right, and thirdly, do the action from a firm and unchangeable character—from the *habit* of doing that kind of action consistently. For Aristotle, it was very important that we develop the moral virtues through habit and practice, doing right actions so that they become part of our identity—our character. *Integrity* is the modern name we use to describe the actions of those persons who consistently act from a firmly established character pattern, doing the right thing. We especially stress the concepts of integrity when there is temptation to diverge from what good character demands. Persons of integrity do not stray from acting in accordance with strong moral principle even when it is expedient or personally advantageous to do so. Persons of integrity act like the ideal persons they are trying to be. This is perhaps what the ancient Taoist has in mind when he says, "The way to do, is to be." Thus the wholeness of the good person, the total identity, is what we mean when we refer to his or her integrity. When we say, "don't sacrifice your integrity" we really mean, "don't stop being who you ought to be."

If I'm a member of one of the professions, then "who I ought to be" must also involve my social role as a practicing professional. My *professional integrity* will include the role specific obligations and responsibilities of my particular profession. I stress here the social character of professional integrity because the community is involved at every stage of professional development.

First of all, the very existence of the professions results from some fundamental need that society has and it is likely to be an eternal need. The need that we have for health care, for example, is unlikely to go away, and it is that need that over time has generated what we know today as the medical profession. It may come as a surprise to some to learn that the health care professions do not exist for the sole purpose of providing employment to health care professionals or profits for health care organizations. It is because of societal need that our communities develop and maintain medical schools and nursing schools. Similarly, every organized society will express its interest in *justice* by providing some variation of a court system and a legal profession. We need an ordered society; we want to be treated fairly; we seek justice. We train our judges and our lawyers in law schools supported by the community because of the important value that we place on justice. Similarly, we know how crucial education is to our society, so we provide for the training of teachers; we know how important security is to our nation-state, so we provide military academies and military training for the members of the military profession.

No member of the professions can escape these ties to the community since they constitute the very reason for the existence of the professions. Thus, professional integrity begins with this necessary responsibility to serve the fundamental need of the community. Notice that the community makes possible the opportunity for one to become qualified in a given profession and usually allows the professionals the authority themselves to set the standards of competence and conduct of its members. Doctors control the licensing and certifying of doctors, lawyers do the same for members of the legal profession, and military officers certify and control the commissioning process for leaders of the military profession.

Members of the public professions are thus educated and supported by the society because of the critical services the professions provide. In the case of teachers in public institutions and in the case of the military profession, practitioners are supported from the public coffers during their entire careers. Clearly, some of the role specific obligations are based on this relationship and on the authority to act on behalf of the entire society which is literally bestowed on these professionals. With the authority to act goes the public trust and violations of that trust are serious breaches of professional integrity. For example, there were instances recently in the local public school systems where two male high school teachers engaged in sexual intimacies with teenaged female students. These teachers violated the trust they had been given, and they violated their professional integrity. But let us direct our attention to the elements of professional integrity in the military profession to see if that will illuminate both our responsibilities as military practitioners and the relationships between professional and personal integrity.

Professional integrity derives its substance from the fundamental goals or mission of the profession. For the military profession we might broadly describe that mission as the preservation and protection of a way of life deemed worth preserving. Just as in medicine one violates professional integrity by performing surgical procedures that are not medically indicated in order to increase the surgeon's income, so too engaging in operations that are not militarily necessary in order to reflect glory on the commander would also be a breach of professional integrity. Killing unarmed prisoners, executing the elderly and babies who are not engaged in the attempt to destroy you is surely inconsistent with the goals of the military and hence a breach of professional integrity.

In the military, as in all of the professions, the issue of *competence* is directly relevant to professional integrity. Because human life, national security, and expenditures from the national treasury are so frequently at issue when the military acts, the obligation to be competent is not merely prudential. That obligation is a moral one and culpable incompetence here is clearly a violation of professional integrity. When a B-52 pilot is known to engage in unsafe practices, when he frequently endangers the lives of other aircrew members and people on the ground by performing forbidden flying maneuvers, then not only does he violate professional integrity, so do those colleagues and superiors who tolerate this conduct and take no action to prevent it. This aspect of professional integrity is worth noting.

Part of the social aspect of professional integrity involves the joint responsibility for conduct and competence shared by all members of the profession. When fellow surgeons bury the mistakes of their incompetent colleagues rather than expose these colleagues and remove their license to practice they fall short of their responsibilities to the goals of the profession—they sin against professional integrity. Only fellow professionals are capable of evaluating competence in some instances and hence, fellow professionals must accept the responsibility of upholding the standards of the profession. Fellow officers can spot derelictions of duty, failures of leadership, failures of competence, and the venalities of conduct that interfere with the goals of the military mission. The wing commanders of that B-52 pilot who knew of his repeated safety violations and failed to ground him before he killed himself and others, failed in their responsibilities—they violated their professional integrity. Often the obligations of professional integrity may be pitted against personal loyalties or friendships, and where the stakes for society are so high, professional integrity should win out.

These lessons seem obvious in theory but are most difficult to put into practice, especially in the preprofessional training which takes place in military academies, medical schools, and law schools. Nontoleration of failures of professional integrity does not seem so crucial in training situations where the stakes are not too high. Perhaps this is why the penalties for tolerating lapses of integrity are ameliorated in training situations but then often seem sensationally tragic when enforced in the professional context. But preprofessionals must learn the importance of the social elements of professional integrity and the responsibility they inherit to maintain standards of competence and conduct in the entire profession and not just for themselves. Society provides the training opportunities, the resources necessary for carrying out the professional function, and the authority to act on its behalf. With this authority to act and the autonomy which usually accompanies it, breaches of professional integrity must be viewed as a serious failure of the societal trust. When a cadet at the Air Force Academy knows that a fellow cadet has plagiarized a paper to meet a deadline and takes no action to correct this behavior, he or she has violated societal trust in a fashion analogous to the colleagues who took no action to correct the unsafe B-52 pilot. If our preprofessional preparation does not inculcate the habits of professional integrity, can we have confidence that those habits will be practiced by these same individuals when they become licensed professionals?

We derive other aspects of professional integrity as we examine the basic functions of each profession. If in preserving our way of life we must use the military instrument, then members of the military profession must sometimes go to war. If combat occurs then professional soldiers must fight. To refuse a combat assignment is to break faith with all other members of the profession and is a first order violation of professional integrity. It would be the equivalent of a teacher refusing to teach, a doctor abandoning patients, a judge refusing to hear crucial cases. Because the stakes are so high in the military case, this breach of professional integrity could be devastating to society.

How are personal integrity and professional integrity related? There are varying opinions about this. Some people believe that one can live up to high standards of competence and conduct in one's professional role—at the hospital, in the school, at the military base—but live an entirely different kind of moral life outside the professional context in one's private life. Some think they may be required to do things in their roles as professionals that they would never do as private laypersons. Some instances of this dichotomy are obvious. As a private person I would normally not even contemplate harming other persons, yet as a military professional I am licensed to kill (under specified conditions) for reasons of state. A variation of this concern surfaced during an annual meeting of the Colorado Bar Association in the fall of 1995. One of the topics offered for small group discussion was the following one: "I would never do many of the things in my personal life that I have to do as a lawyer." At the heart of this matter is the issue of client advocacy. Lawyers are enjoined to act in their clients' interests and to do so zealously. In defending my rapist client whom I know to be guilty, I may cross examine the innocent rape victim in such a fashion as to totally discredit her even though I know she is telling the truth. If it is legal and will help my client, it would seem that the standards of the profession require me to do it, even though in ordinary morality I would judge it to be wrong to harm an innocent person.[1] This sort of example really is problematic for it appears to reveal a direct conflict between personal integrity and professional integrity.

There are similar examples in medicine. Abortion for convenience is legally permitted in most U.S. hospitals, but some obstetricians believe that convenience abortions are immoral so in these hospitals they find a conflict between professional integrity and personal integrity. Now in most such situations, doctors and nurses are permitted to refuse to participate on moral grounds even though the action itself is legally permitted. Perhaps this is one key to resolving integrity dilemmas—what is legally permitted is not always or even usually morally obligatory. But I mention these possible clashes between professional integrity and personal integrity because I wish to minimize them. I wish to support the view that the two types of integrity are generally compatible and to foster the position that they are interdependent. What I wish to argue is that since professions exist to serve society's need for important values (education, health, justice, security, etc.), the means used to provide those values and services should be morally decent means and the persons in the professions who provide them should be morally decent persons.

Put in more direct terms, good teachers ought to be good persons, good doctors ought to be good persons, good lawyers ought to be good persons, and good military professionals ought to be good persons. We want to live in a world where the duties of a competent professional can be carried out by a good person with a clear and confident conscience. That means that professional practices must always be constrained by basic moral principles. That this is not always the case now is obvious: several of the attorneys at the previously mentioned convention pointed out that they had left certain large law firms because they perceived that they were being asked to do things that violated their personal integrity. Now in the best of all possible worlds, the moral restraints on professional functions would have made those same actions inimical to professional integrity as well. And this is the proper order of things. When professions go beyond their essential service function to society and distort their purpose toward profits, power, or greed then they lose the trust and respect of their communities—they stop being professions. Militarism is the pejorative term we use to describe a society or a military gone bad in the sense that it distorts the essential goals and function of the military profession. The twin sources of guidance we use to hold militarism in check are the just war theories and the laws of war. These twin guides are related in an essential way to professional integrity—they represent in the broadest terms, when and how the military instrument ought to be used.

Well-established professions often spell out the role-specific principles which support that profession's conception of professional integrity. The codes of conduct promulgated by the American Medical Association and the American Bar Association and state and local chapters of these groups are well known. The military profession has many codes, regulations, mottoes, and traditions which combine to form a military ethic on which professional integrity is based. At the Air Force Academy we have our honor code, our honor oath, and our specific list of core values which is now identical with the official list of core values of the Air Force. When we say that we value integrity first, service before self, and excellence in all that we do, we acknowledge that the essential nature of the military profession is to serve our parent society. We make specific our commitment to the conception that good soldiers are good persons. What we should mean when we commit ourselves to "integrity first" is that we understand the importance of both personal integrity and professional integrity and through our efforts to keep them compatible we will best provide the crucial military function to our society.

Note

1. I am indebted to F. A. Elliston's *Ethics and the Legal Profession* (1983) for this example as quoted in T. L. Shaffer's *American Legal Ethics: Text, Readings, and Discussion Topics* (New York: Matthew Bender, 1985), 335.

Part IV

WARFARE: MORAL ISSUES

Chapter 12

MORALITY AND WAR

Absolutes, Universals, and War

If we are to discuss war and morality meaningfully, we should first distinguish between the morality *of* war and morality *in* war. The first issue, the morality of war; has occupied the attention of philosophers for many centuries; but with the advent of modern weapons, it has received renewed critical emphasis. The question of morality in war also has received additional special scrutiny since the Nuremberg trials at the end of World War II. We cannot presume to provide definitive solutions where greater minds have tried and failed, but we must at the minimum discover the moral considerations relevant to the modern forms of war.

What kinds of moral principles can shed some light on the general question of war? Is war intrinsically evil and hence always and everywhere absolutely forbidden? Are some wars morally justified and others not? Some help may be found if we push the question further back for a brief look at our attitudes toward moral principles themselves. Are there *absolute* moral standards; if so, what do they command us to do with respect to war?

Some commonsense reflections may reveal what kinds of absolutes men have subscribed to and what their relationship can be to specific situations. These reflections may incidentally assist us in understanding the so-called new morality or situational morality currently being evaluated by theologians and moralists.

We can view an *absolute* moral principle as one which holds for all rational beings in *all possible* circumstances. Examples of these principles are "One ought always to do good and avoid evil," "Always act in accordance with right reason," and the Kantian categorical imperative (in this formulation) "Act according to that maxim which you can at the same time will to be a universal law." Interestingly enough, these absolute principles have the common characteristic of vagueness—in fact, one may observe that the more acts one attempts to include within the same principle, the less specific it is.

There is a second category of principles which we may refer to meaningfully as *universal* moral principles. Universal principles are those

---

Reprinted with permission from *Man and Value, Essays in Honor of William H. Werkmeister*, edited by E.F. Kaelin, University Presses of Florida, Tallahassee, 1981.

which hold for all rational beings in *analogous* circumstances. Examples of universal principles are "One ought to keep his promises," "One ought to be truthful," "One ought to preserve life wherever possible," "One ought not to steal," "One ought not to kill other human beings," etc. Universal principles are more specific than absolute ones for they refer to act-types.

Now one of the things we insist upon is that our universal principles "fit" or that they be subsumed under our absolute principles. "Promise-keeping" had better be one of those act-types which is "good." But there is a difference between the types of morally obliging principles which we must notice: Absolute obligations, if they are really absolute, must *always* be observed and could never be in conflict with any other absolute obligations since they oblige in all circumstances. On the other hand, universal obligations may and do often conflict; we can conceive of human circumstances in which we are forced to choose between keeping a promise and saving a life. Consider the following homely example: I promise to be home at 6 P.M., but at 5:55 en route I spot an accident with an injured person lying on the road. If I stop I may be able to help save a life, but in order to do so I must break a promise. What I ought to do in this *particular* situation depends on which universal principle, value, or obligation takes precedence in this case here and now. In other words the particular situation is crucially relevant in the determination of my immediate moral duty. This does not mean that either promise-keeping or life-saving must be given up as a universal moral obligation; it does mean that I must make a rational moral decision as to which takes precedence in *this* situation.

An important point to notice again is that my choosing to observe the duty to attempt to preserve life in this case does not mean that we give up the universal duty to keep promises. Promise-keeping is still a universal obligation; it simply yields to what is a higher obligation in these circumstances. One can conceive of other circumstances in which keeping a promise might be the higher obligation. This distinction between absolute and universal moral norms should assist us in clarifying much of the recent controversy over "situation ethics." Moral judgments do require taking account of particular situations, but this requirement is not to be construed as a reduction to subjective relativism in ethics.

We have tried frequently in frustrating ways to make our "absolute" principles do more than they ever could for us—they simply are not specific enough for particular situations. Often enough this is also true of our universal principles. We cannot rid ourselves of the personal responsibility for judging the particular facts of a given situation to determine which of our principles it "fits" under. Perhaps the dignity of being human rests on this crucial personal responsibility. The Church, theologians, moralists, society, the State—all may pronounce judgments concerning absolute or universal principles. But each individual person is responsible for applying that guidance to the complex situations of life that confront him. To attempt to lay down moral prescriptions for each human situation would appear to be both impossible and unnecessary; perhaps this is why Christ himself reacted to the many specific rules of behavior which were laid down by the busy canon-makers and suggested a single, more simple moral law.

If we apply this brief consideration of moral principles to the question of war, we should conclude that the obligation to avoid war is a universal obligation just as the obligation to avoid killing other human beings is a universal obligation. Killing another person can be and traditionally has been viewed as morally justified when the obligation to avoid this action conflicts with another universal obligation which in a particular situation takes precedence. Arguments for killing in self-defense, to protect the threatened life of an innocent person, and to protect society against convicted criminals all seem to rest ultimately on this form of justification. A brief review of classical attempts to distinguish "just" from "unjust" wars suggests a marked similarity of approach.

For several centuries, Christian moralists held that a war was "just" if it was initiated by legitimate state authority for a just cause with the right intention and employed the right use of means. These conditions were modified in modern times by Pope Pius XII and since then have been reevaluated by many lay and theological thinkers. Catholic moral theology prior to Pius XII, for example, included under "just causes" for going to war the retaking of territory conquered by an enemy, redress for a serious injustice, protection of religion, and defense of nations against oppression.[1] Plus XII clarified the concept of "grave injustice" by excluding the violation of minor rights, national prestige, etc., as not constituting grounds sufficient for declaring war. He emphasized both the position that war is a "last resort" and the principle of limitation in the use of force. Much more emphasis was placed on the principle of proportion; i.e., the damage already endured by the aggression must be weighed against the damage likely to be caused by a war initiated to redress the injustice. Further, careful consideration must be given to the proportion between the evils caused by war and the real probability of success.[2]

More recently, John Courtney Murray maintained that the current application of the classical just war doctrines demands observance of the following two principles:

> (1) All wars of aggression, whether just or unjust, fall under the ban of moral prescription.
> (2) A defensive war against unjust aggression is morally admissible both in principle and in fact.[3]

These basic moral norms are consistent with the legal agreements contained in the Covenant of the League of Nations, the Kellogg-Briand Pact (1928), and the condemnation of aggressive war contained in the judgments at Nuremberg and embodied in the United Nations Charter.

Robert W. Tucker, in his study of contemporary American doctrines of war,[4] suggests essentially that most recent public pronouncements on the just war by American statesmen have maintained that "the just war is the war fought either in self-defense or in collective defense against an armed attack."[5] This position is roughly in agreement with the principles enunciated by Murray and carries with it a moral condemnation of any preventive or preemptive war since such wars would have to be labeled "aggression" on the part of the initiator. Tucker attributes the general "American" position on just war (which is also viewed as "lawful" war) to such spokesmen as Roosevelt, Stimson, Wilson, Truman, Eisenhower, and Dulles. Tucker goes on to point out the complex difficulties inherent in maintaining self-defense as the only justification for war, but we shall have to leave these considerations for another discussion.[6] We should take note in passing, however, that nations engaged in modern wars have protested loudly that the enemy was the aggressor; and this has been maintained even by those nations who actually initiated the fighting.

Returning to our earlier remarks about the nature of "universal" as distinguished from "absolute" moral principles, we can note that the conditions which have been adduced for making war a permissible and justifiable act both in the past and in contemporary positions are conditions which specify certain universal principles which may take precedence over the universal principle to avoid war. Conditions like "last resort," "proper proportion," "self-defense," etc., all seem to be aimed at what our commonsense reflections suggested must be evaluated in choosing among conflicting moral obligations.

There are many contemporary thinkers, however, who have adopted the position that the prohibition against war must become an *absolute* moral norm. The frightening destructive power now available, the negotiating instrument of the United Nations forum, and trends toward recognition of international agreements as legally binding on nations, all argue that war must be absolutely condemned as a means of national or international policy. Recognizing man's natural competitiveness as well as his acquisitiveness, however, others have argued that we need a moral equivalent of war to drain off man's natural drives and energies. Still others have argued convincingly that neither international law nor negotiations through the United Nations have yet reached a stage to be relied upon for the settlement of national differences. To deny the right of self-defense to any government is to raise the whole question of the right of a given society to exist as a self-determined state. Even given the formal and effective establishment of a world government, we can envision questions being raised concerning the right of revolution and the "justness" of civil wars. Given the nature of absolute moral principles, namely, that they must be observed in all possible circumstances, it would seem difficult in our present world to defend the elevation of the prohibition of all war from a universal to an absolute moral norm.

Morality *in* War

Let us turn for a moment to the question of morality *in* war as distinguished from the more general issue of the morality *of* war. Moral issues *in* war involve the use of means, the identification and treatment of noncombatants, the treatment of prisoners, conscientious objection, assessment of war crimes, etc. Perhaps the one recurrent moral theme to emerge from our war experiences in this century is that all is *not* fair in war. Our nation and almost all other nations have publicly subscribed to the view that there are legal and moral restrictions on the means to be employed in war and on the permissible behavior of man toward man even in war. As history has revealed over and over again, however, public agreement has not prevented men from violating both legal and moral behavior norms or governments from violating those agreements when it was expedient to do so in their own interest.

Much has been written concerning the use of nuclear weapons, biological and chemical warfare, bombing of cities which have no military or industrial facilities, and in general the means which are morally and legally permissible to achieve victory in battle. Modern weapons have made it extremely difficult for moralists and theologians to remain perfectly clear in their analysis of the time-honored distinction between combatants and noncombatants. It is not obvious that we can add much to the ongoing agonizing discussion of these issues. But events in the struggle for control of Vietnam as well as current violence in Northern Ireland and the Middle East have focused attention on some moral issues in war which strain the very limits of our most discerning moral judges. Because of their contemporary sensitivity and the lack of authoritative moral guidance we must approach these problems with even more humility than the more general issues already mentioned.

We can find very little assistance from our moral guides of the past in evaluating the moral implications of the violence instigated in *undeclared* wars. Are the permissible moral conditions for revolutions analogous to those for wars in general? If so, in today's world can we discern when a people would be acting defensively if they are to revolt against their established government? How are we to evaluate the various guerrilla attacks in the Middle East and the street bombings in Northern Ireland? Were the deaths of Israeli Olympic athletes in Munich the result of a legitimate act of war? Is the "execution" of a village leader in Vietnam a legitimate act of war, or is it a murder of a noncombatant? Is a guerrilla who bombs a theater in Saigon, crowded with women and children, to be viewed in the same moral light as a pilot who drops a bomb on a village which he knows has no armed troops in it? It seems apparent that guerrilla warfare and "wars of liberation," while remaining below the level of a universally feared nuclear holocaust, have nevertheless generated a host of different moral problems.

Incidents like the killings in My Lai in March of 1968 and the mass executions of civilians in Hue the preceding month have commanded great attention in the public press and in the moral consciences of many Americans. The issues raised in My Lai have caused us to look more thoroughly at the question of illegal or immoral orders and the individual responsibilities of every soldier. More stress has been placed on the observance of the basic moral precepts regarding the treatment of prisoners contained in the Geneva Convention and the Army rules of land warfare. The mass executions at Hue did not provoke the clamor that My Lai did, perhaps because not as much was clearly known, perhaps because Americans were not so involved. But the moral issue is one which is of crucial significance with respect to what is permissible in this new form of war.

On January 26, 1968, the chief members of the Hue City Committee of the Communist Party drew up the final plan for targeting their missions in Hue as part of the Tet Offensive. The first goal of that plan in roughly verbatim translation was as follows:

> Destroy and disorganize the enemy's restrictive administrative machinery from the province and district levels to city wards, streets and wharves. To pursue until the end spies, reactionaries, and reactionaries who exploit Catholics in and outside the country *[sic]*. To prevent them from escaping and to punish scoundrels, hoodlums, and robbers who kill the people and disturb peace and honor.[7]

Specific families were targeted to accomplish the destruction of the administrative support for the "enemy"; and during the twenty-five days the North Vietnamese and Viet Cong occupied the city of Hue, they used their black lists to lead off and execute more than 2,800 civilians, most of whose bodies were gradually uncovered in mass grave sites, several having been buried alive. In Oberdorfer's authentic reporting of these events in the book *Tet!,* he states that "it is clear from the overwhelming weight of evidence that this was for the most part a deliberate slaughter, ordered from on high for plain and specific purposes."[8] General Giap is reported to have sent word to the Hue Committee that the battle of Hue was "an unprecedented victory of scientific quality," and Premier Pham Van Dong is quoted as having said "the battle was the greatest success in the people's revolution in South Vietnam." These facts were reported by Oberdorfer[9] along with the following quotation from a Communist report: "The most outstanding feature was that we won an overall success, militarily and politically. This was a typical example of our tactic on how to occupy and defend a city."

These details concerning the executions at Hue have been included here in order to identify more clearly that this action was viewed by its perpetrators as a legitimate means of waging war. Obviously, on this view of modern guerrilla warfare there is no distinction possible between uniformed and nonuniformed enemy; there are no noncombatants. My personal moral judgments confirm the rightness of our search for those responsible for violating our legal and moral norms at My Lai. Moral consistency also demands the condemnation of the "execution" of civilians in guerrilla thrusts like those at Hue. If this was indeed "a typical example of . . . how to occupy and defend a city" and is to be pursued by the leaders of one of the world's nations, then it demands the immediate attention of and evaluation by our greatest moral thinkers and international legal authorities. Can this tactic of killing unarmed civilians be morally condoned at the same time that we concern ourselves about the moral rights of prisoners of war who have actually participated in the shooting war? And what may we expect will befall the losers of any war in which this tactic is a "typical example"?

In recent years many concerned thinkers have argued that the destructive means available in nuclear weapons make it impossible to maintain the distinction between combatants and noncombatants. Even those who maintain that wars can only be morally permissible if fought in self-defense must, on the view of nuclear pacifism, admit that where sufficient nuclear weapons are employed even as a deterrent, the will to use them must involve a violation of "right intention." Right intention, in the classical "just war" formulation, forbids the destruction or even the threat of the destruction of the entire opposing society; genocide is viewed as morally wrong. Since right intention involves avoidance of harm to noncombatants, and this seems manifestly impossible where strategic nuclear weapons are to be employed in sufficient quantities to constitute a deterrent force, then, say the nuclear pacifists, there can be no legitimate claim even to self-defense. Others, including John Courtney Murray[10] and Theodore Weber[11] argued that this state of affairs shows that the theory of just wars must be reevaluated so that its contemporary relevance can in fact be seen. Murray argues that, properly used, the just war theory can help us to refute a number of false dilemmas, like the extreme choices between war and morality or between "being red and being dead." Weber suggests that the relevance of just war theory for modern warfare can be recovered by reversing the "usual pattern of moral inquiry."

> Customarily, the procedure is from politics to war. War is the "last resort" when the attempts to secure justice through political means have failed. And as "last resort" it must yet be conducted justly. Now we must proceed from war to politics, because both "last resort" and the violation of just conduct are present in principle in the countervailing weapons systems of major nuclear powers.[12]

Lt. General Sir John Winthrop Hackett, blending the voice of military experience with a morally sensitive wisdom, also sees the need for reevaluating our use of the terms "war" and "peace" in a world assessing the means for its own total destruction.

> If by war, we still mean total war as Clausewitz did, war can no longer be what Clausewitz called it—the continuation of policy by other means. It is difficult to argue … that unrestricted war between powers of high and roughly equal nuclear capability can possibly be brought about by a rational act of deliberate policy. General war can result, it seems to me, from miscalculation, or aberration or mischance… War in the sense of general unrestricted war, however, can no longer be regarded as a normal continuation of foreign policy or an alternative to peace.… What is required … is the ability to deploy that degree of warlike effort which the circumstances demand, in gentle gradation from something very small to something which though pretty large, is still short of general mobilization…. War, total war, we have to avoid. Warfare, acts of organized violence between groups of men which in sum amount to less than total war, which we are unlikely to be able entirely to prevent, we must do something about.[13]

This mention of the moral difficulties inherent in even a defensive posture where nuclear deterrence is involved as a strategy is made here because one can perceive a parallel difficulty even in "limited" wars of insurgency as demonstrated by the mass executions in Hue. Both insurgents and counterinsurgents operate as a matter of strategy among the people. Insurgents make use of the people for providing supplies, concealment, proselytizing, intelligence information, etc. Further, insurgents use selected terror directly against noncombatant members of the existing civil structure. They frequently wear no uniforms. The identification of a "military" target becomes almost totally impossible in this type of warfare. The principle of immunity for noncombatants is almost as problematical as in the case of nuclear strategy, though on a reduced scale. Is the insurgent morally wrong because he does in fact frequently target against the people in the civilian structure rather than the military? Is the counterinsurgent wrong when he attacks a village which shelters and supplies the insurgents? Should British soldiers fire back when Irish snipers fire at them from buildings or crowds containing "uninvolved" civilians? And what is the status of those who are ordinary workers by day and guerrilla fighters by night?

Other problems receiving new focus include the question of conscientious objection. Many countries have recognized and made special provision for the primacy of conscience with respect to the general requirement for citizens to fight in their country's wars. In the United States, our most recent Supreme Court ruling has liberalized the grounds for conscientious objection as a legal position, but has not permitted that status to be claimed by those who object on moral or religious grounds to fighting in a specific war as distinguished from objecting to fighting in all wars. There have been several well-publicized cases of military men on active duty, both officers and enlisted men, who have refused to accept orders to Vietnam on grounds of conscience. These cases are subject to analysis in terms of a conflict of universal obligations. Each military man assumes the universal obligation to obey all legal orders of his superiors when he takes his oath of office and/or accepts his commission. Each man at the same time has a universal obligation to disobey illegal or immoral orders. In the absence of clear evidence to the contrary one may assume that his orders are both legal and moral. However, as the fighting in Vietnam continued over several years, more and more American citizens, many in high legislative positions, questioned the length, the legality, and the morality of the United States' involvement. This state of affairs caused many men severe trauma in their attempts to make a clear moral judgment in resolving their conflicting universal obligations in a context which did not appear to them to be clear at all. The very existence of such moral sensitivity, much of it totally and obviously sincere, can be viewed as a commentary both on man's moral progress and on the sheer moral complexity that forms of modern warfare evoke.

Who Decides?

We have seen the difficult moral perplexities that attend any serious considerations of the decisions to be made concerning modern warfare. Clearly, a mere consideration of these difficulties does not resolve them nor does it, by itself, eliminate the possibility that men and governments will continue to make war on each other. It seems obvious, however, that the moral issues raised here must be of paramount concern to those men who represent their governments in arms limitation talks, to those men who have been empowered by their constituents to commit their nations to participate in wars, and to those men who are asked to fight in war and to whose care are entrusted the awesome weapons of modern arsenals.

Plato's idealistic remark in Book VII of the *Republic* concerning philosophers and politics seems more relevant than ever. The decision to go to war is more than ever a moral as well as a political decision, and political leaders must of necessity concern themselves with moral philosophy. Decisions to use modern weapons are more than ever moral decisions and not merely military strategies. Tactics of an insurgent or counterinsurgent movement embrace political, military, and moral complexities. Who shall we trust to make these crucial decisions for us? Professional philosophers may well continue to evaluate the actions of nations and men from afar and after decisions have been made, but will their reflections have a bearing on the decisions themselves? Only if the political leaders who make decisions *about* war are themselves maturely attuned to the philosophical implications of their choices for all mankind. Only if the military leaders who make decisions in war are both intellectually and morally capable of assessing the total implications of their actions. In a world where primary emphasis is being placed on the dignity of our individual existence simultaneously with the will of many to use violence in asserting or subverting that right to personal dignity, it is no longer possible for philosophers to maintain an external, perhaps clinical, aloofness. We can no longer endure the separation of the political from the philosophical nor the military from the moral.

Notes

1. Dr. Karl Hörmann, *Peace and Modern War in the Judgment of the Church,* trans. Caroline Hemesath (Westminister, Md.: Newman Press, 1966), 41 ff.

2. John Courtney Murray, *Morality and Modern War* (New York: The Council on Religion and International Affairs, 1959), 12-13.

3. Murray, *Morality and Modern War*, 9-10.

4. Robert W. Tucker, *The Just War* (Baltimore: The Johns Hopkins Press,1960).

5. Tucker, *The Just War*, 11.

6. In my recent anthology, *War, Morality, and the Military Profession* (Boulder, CO: Westview Press, 1979), this and several related issues receive extensive treatment from a number of contemporary thinkers.

7. Don Oberdorfer, *Tet!* (New York: Doubleday & Co., 1971), 206.

8. Oberdorfer, *Tet!*, 232.

9. Oberdorfer, *Tet!*, 231.

10. Murray, *Morality and Modern War*, see especially 15 ff.

11. Theodore R. Weber, *Modern War and the Pursuit of Peace* (New York: The Council on Religion and International Affairs, 1968), esp.15 ff.

12. Weber, *Modern War*, 24.

13. Lt. Gen. Sir John Winthrop Hackett, *The Profession of Arms* (London: The Times Publishing Co. Ltd., 1962), 55-56.

Chapter 13

GOD OR GUNS: A FALSE DICHOTOMY

"Ought a country that considers itself a Christian nation depend on its armament for protection or ought it to depend upon God for its protection?"

This question, as proposed for discussion at this conference, seems intended to be interpreted as an exclusive disjunction; that is, either you rely on God or you rely on guns, and you must opt for one or the other but not both. This would be an unfortunate dilemma for religious citizens if indeed the only available choices are so construed, but these are not exclusive choices nor the only choices, as I hope to demonstrate in the discussion which follows.

Absolute Pacifism

There are those who would argue that the use of force against other human beings is always and everywhere forbidden by the teachings of Christ. They may be grouped with those who for religious or nonreligious reasons believe it morally wrong ever to use force against other persons, even to resist the violent aggression of other persons. I will call this view "absolute pacifism." It is a pacifism that admits of no exceptions, either on a personal or a national level. Any protection provided to the "innocent" victim of aggressive violence, on this view, must be provided by God, unaided by humans employing force.

It is my contention that absolute pacifism is an unreasonable position both from an understanding of the nature of human existence and from the perspective of Christianity. To deny the use of force to some legitimized arm of society is perhaps to abandon the very possibility of an ordered society, but this position will be pursued in depth later on in the discussion. First, let's examine absolute pacifism as possibly dictated by the traditional teachings of Christianity.

Presented in Albuquerque, NM, at the "Science, Philosophy and Religion Symposium," January 1982. Published in the proceedings of that symposium.

In the sermon on the mount we are told that the meek and the peacemakers among men are blessed. Surely we can appreciate these counsels of prudence and incorporate them in our lives, but can we derive from them an absolute prohibition against the use of force? The Christian pacifist points to these counsels, to the injunctions to "resist not evil," to "turn the other cheek" and to "love our enemies," and concludes that Christ has ordered him (and the rest of us) to be pacifist. Yet, as Elizabeth Anscombe has pointed out,[1] Christ does not condemn the military life nor others who are commissioned by societal authority to use force in maintaining order. Indeed, in the episode with the centurion who asked Christ to heal his servant, we do not find Christ rebuking the officer for being in the military; rather we find him commending this Roman soldier for his faith. If the military profession were evil in itself, if the use of force for the purpose of maintaining order was condemned by Christ, then this encounter with the centurion must be viewed as extremely curious! Anscombe suggests that:

> On a pacifist view, this must be much as if a madam in a brothel had said: "I know what authority is, I tell this girl to do this and she does it" and Christ had commended her faith.[2]

Perhaps the important observation to make is that those who attempt to derive support for absolute pacifism from the *New Testament* have too narrow a view of Christianity which counts as sacred scripture also the *Old Testament* and which derives its total moral position from these sources and the teaching tradition of the Christian church over several centuries. We are indebted to Anscombe for pointing out as well that in the traditions of the Judeo-Christian ethic we find realistic characterizations of evil in the world but not an evil that is permitted free rein against all legitimate authority.

> We are taught that God retains the evil will of the devil within limits by violence: we are not given a picture of God permitting to the devil all that he is capable of. There is currently a conception of Christianity as having revealed that the defeat of evil must always be by pure love without coercion; this at least is shown to be false by the foregoing consideration. And without the alleged revelation there could be no reason to believe such a thing.[3]

Many of the very early followers of Christ believed that "the kingdom of God is at hand" in a very literal sense; they expected the end of the world to occur in their lifetime. For some of those in that circumstance, pacifism made a great deal of sense, although many soldiers are also numbered among the early Christian martyrs (martyrs not because they refused to fight but because they refused to subscribe to non-Christian beliefs). But as the church matured and expanded, its principal theologians and teachers developed a position on war, known as just-war theory, that takes into account a rational stewardship for this world, a stewardship that includes responsibility for defending the polity against external aggressors.

We need to examine the classical just-war position very critically; but before doing so, it may be worth observing "absolute pacifism" as it occurs in the adherents of at least one other religion. Perhaps the most famous advocate of nonviolence as a method of resisting oppression was Mahatma Gandhi of India. According to one of his biographers,[4] Gandhi was "delighted" with the message of Christ's sermon on the mount which he likened to the *Bhagavad-Gita*, a "gospel" of Hinduism. Remarkably enough, the *Bhagavad-Gita* ("*Song of God*") is an epic poem relating a conversation on a battlefield. Krishna, an incarnation of Vishnu (god, the preserver), explains to Arjuna, leader of one of the contending armies in a civil war, that it is the duty of a warrior to fight with courage and to set aside his reservations against killing in a righteous war. In the process of the long conversation Krishna delineates much of the Hindu doctrine of reincarnation, the types of yoga, the duties of caste, and the importance of renouncing externals in the search for god within man's inner self. The *Gita* must be set against the important Hindu doctrine of *ahimsa*, which enjoins against the killing of all living things. How is one to find a consistent position in these seemingly conflicting views of war? Gandhi, unlike many other Hindus, interpreted the *Gita* as a lengthy allegory with Arjuna representing man's struggle against evil in his own soul which is the battlefield that counts.[5]

Is it possible that a great insight lies just beyond our grasp regarding these issues as they occur both in the *New Testament* and in the *Bhagavad-Gita*? Are there two views of man for us to contend with: one, a view of man in his spiritual existence attempting to work out his individual salvation, his soul's ultimate relationship with God; and second, a view of man in human society, caught up in a physical world which involves working and eating, marriage and politics, peace and war? Can "the kingdom of God is at hand" be a message for each individual to heed in his own lifetime with regard to giving primacy to his moral and spiritual life and not an immediate apocalyptic message for the universe as a whole? Is the problem of human existence really the problem of reaching a balance between citizenship in the "city of God" and citizenship in the "city of man"?

The Just War Tradition

Beginning with Augustine and including the works of Aquinas, Suarez, Bellarmine, Vitoria, and Grotius, there evolved through the medieval period a theory dealing with warfare which has come to be known as just-war theory and identified as a Christian teaching (Grotius is the only nontheologian in the list mentioned above). While these thinkers recognized war as a physical evil, they acknowledged that nations may sometimes be morally permitted or even morally obligated to wage war under certain conditions. Essentially, they argued that men or nations who use military power for evil purposes are not to be allowed to pursue their aims unchecked when they violate the rights of other persons or nations (rights to life, property, sovereignty, territorial integrity, etc.).

Borrowing liberally from Aristotle, Aquinas and other Christian theologians following him perceived society as "natural" to man. That is to say, as man appears in the world (on their view, as created by God), he cannot survive on his own—human society is a necessary element in God's creative act, and this can be learned by mere observation. Thus the family is a natural structure, intended for the nurture, education, and protection of family members with natural and necessary authority resting with parents. Similarly the state is a natural institution, intended to nurture, educate, and protect its citizens, and deriving its authority and responsibility from the citizens themselves who in turn acquired that authority and responsibility from the creative God who constituted them with the ability to reason and choose. Laws which the state promulgates and enforces carry legitimacy, but only if they are aimed at the common good since their authority derives from each member of the society. The authority to bind the whole society rests with those authorized to do so by the members. Thus responsibility for maintaining order in the society and authority to enforce laws rests with established governmental agents, not with private individuals.

Given this view of the polity, the Christian just-war theorist must find the choice between God and guns implied by our initial discussion question to be a false dichotomy. Given its authority and responsibility for the well-being of its citizens (and that authority ultimately coming from God), the state is surely permitted and perhaps obligated to protect its citizens both from internal and from external attack. And it does so acting under authority derived ultimately from God. Order and harmony in society is its intended natural state; disruption of order, whether it be by criminal activity or attack by an external enemy, is an interference which needs to be corrected by the only agency authorized to use force legitimately—the agency charged with the care of the entire community.

Since criminals abound in the present world, and since they frequently attack their victims with weapons of violence, it seems clear that those charged with protecting citizens from criminals must be permitted the use of force or they cannot carry out their function. Anscombe provides a succinct summary of this view of the need to authorize societal guardians to use force. She says:

> To think that society's coercive authority is evil is akin to thinking the flesh evil and family life evil. These things belong to the present constitution of mankind; and if the exercise of coercive power is a manifestation of evil, and not just the means of restraining it, then human nature is totally depraved in a manner never taught by

> Christianity. For society is essential to human good; and society without coercive power is generally impossible.[6]

Thus it is, that the first principle adduced in just-war theory frequently is that war must be declared by *legitimate authority* (those who have the care of the entire state). The remaining conditions that are frequently included if a war is to be viewed as "just" are that it must have a *just cause*, be pursued for the *right intention*, and employ *just means*. Over time, other conditions were added to assure that a nation would be morally justified in going to war. A just cause must include the attempt to right some prior wrong; the resort to war to correct that wrong must be a *last resort* after nonviolent attempts to correct the wrong have failed. There must be *some chance of success*; since the natural state of human society is thought to be that of ordered harmony, war is waged only to restore a just peace. Conditions for the justified warring nation must have some chance of being better after the fighting ends. Further, the concept of *proportionality* plays an important role in determining the nature of war: the harm already endured must be weighed against the physical evil likely to be caused by fighting a war to correct the initial harm. Through each of these just war conditions runs an underlying theme which has been made explicit in a host of international treaties: the rights of innocent noncombatants must be protected even in war.

The development of just-war theory by Christian theologians and moral philosophers has been motivated by concern for justice on an international scale and by the obviously felt need to impose restraint upon the warring parties. The attitude of the absolute pacifist previously described may generate far more evil (both moral and physical) in the world than that of the just-war theorist. Viewing all killing as wrong, the pacifist attitude may lead to lack of discrimination when fighting does in fact occur. Once engaged in evil enterprise, the pacifist attitude does not observe proportionality or protection of the innocent and ignores restraint on the use of means. Since that attitude views all war to be evil, it rejects any "rules of war" and seeks to conclude the fighting as quickly as possible even if that involves inflicting enormous losses on enemy civilians. The pacifist attitude may insidiously distort the reasoning of those who fight; convinced that killing human beings is always wrong, and that God is on their side, they view the enemy as nonhuman, and they wage a "holy war" against the forces of evil. The failure to accept a distinction between the justified use of force by those authorized to act on behalf of the entire society and the unjust use of force against the innocent has led to more evil in the world, perhaps, than the attempts of just-war theorists to introduce rational conditions constraining human warfare.

Enter Technology

Not all modern pacifists are "absolute" pacifists. With the advent of nuclear weapons, many contemporary moral philosophers and theologians have argued that just-war theory no longer applies. While these "nuclear pacifists" might maintain that some wars are justified, they are overwhelmed by the possible consequences for mankind of a nuclear holocaust. They see no possible way of meeting the conditions of proper proportion, right use of means, or right intentions (including the intention to observe the rights of noncombatants), and hence can envision no cause that could justify the initiation of a war involving the use of nuclear weapons.

The nuclear pacifist does not necessarily reject all uses of force. He can agree that legitimate societal authorities may use force to protect society from criminals within; indeed, in an era of rising crime rates the constabulary function may be seen as critical. It is his great concern that modern weapons of war cannot be used discriminately because of their vast explosive power, radioactive fallout, etc., that causes him to reject war altogether. This, of course, is to assume that modern war must be total war and involve an exchange of the most devastating sort. But our choices are not restricted to total war or no war. The world we experience today cannot be described as one at peace—nor is it in a state of total war. The distinction between peace and war has become very blurred. How shall we describe conditions in 1981 in Afghanistan, in Iran and Iraq, in parts of Africa, in Lebanon, in Northern Ireland, in Cambodia? Does either the term "peace" or the term "war" accurately explain the status of these parts of our world?

Clearly, warfare—military fighting—is going on in the world at the present time and seems likely to occur continuously or at least intermittently in the future. Perhaps General Hackett has perceived most accurately what a rational posture toward war today must be when he tells us that total war (general unrestricted war) can no longer be viewed as a rational alternative to peace.[7] Rather, he says:

> What is required is the ability to deploy that degree of warlike effort that the circumstances demand, in general gradation from something very small to something that, though large, is still short of general mobilization…War, total war, we have to avoid. Warfare, acts of organized violence between groups of men which in sum amount to less than total war, which we are unlikely to be able entirely to prevent, we must do something about.[8]

Hackett goes on to agree with Morris Janowitz[9] that the principal function of our military forces must become a constabulary one, using force in a timely fashion to contain violence at the lowest level possible. "The main purpose of the profession of arms," he tells us, "is not to win wars but to avoid them." Warfare, viewed as limited in this fashion, is not a "last resort" but takes on a function very analogous to the internal police function of nation-states.

The concept of military force as a "last resort" is an intriguing one to pursue in an era of nuclear deterrence. Paskins and Dockrill, in their recent book entitled *The Ethics of War*[10] suggest that the policy of nuclear deterrence has radically changed the previously held just-war principle of last resort. They point out that prior to World Wars I and II, the military was viewed as the last resort when other means of conducting international politics failed. After 1945 the military element in the form of nuclear deterrence was no longer a last resort but an essential aspect of keeping peace. Between the world wars, the League of Nations was viewed as a possible guarantor of peace, but after 1945 that role was assumed by a policy of nuclear deterrence. Obviously "guarantor of peace" in this sense uses the term "peace" as opposed to "total war" since it is clear that neither the current structure of the United Nations nor nuclear deterrence have deterred warfare of a limited nature.

This perspective, viewing nuclear deterrence as a guarantor of peace, not only suggests the need for a critical reexamination of the conditions associated with just-war theory today but also places a sharper focus on the "God or guns" topic of this symposium. Should we rely on an umbrella of nuclear deterrence as the method for preventing total war while using the military instrument to contain all other fighting at the lowest possible level? Would a world in which the United States alone or the United States and the U.S.S.R. together eliminated all of their nuclear weapons be a more stable world than the one we have now? How does nuclear proliferation bear on this issue? Clearly, nuclear deterrence as the guarantor of peace (as opposed to total war) assumes that actors on the international scene who control the nuclear weapons are rational agents. But with proliferation of modern technology, who can safely predict that the knowledge to produce weapons of mass destruction will remain with persons or nations who are eminently rational?

Perhaps the single most difficult issue for the morally sensitive citizen of our time to consider is the dilemma which a posture of nuclear deterrence poses. From the point of view of a U.S. citizen, our ability to provide retaliatory nuclear strikes against any overt massive act of aggression has deterred potential aggressors for many years from initiating actions that could culminate in total war. Yet, to carry out the retaliatory act itself, particularly if doing so were to involve the destruction of large population centers, would be to violate the underlying theme of the just-war conditions of proper proportion, chance of success, and protection of the innocent.

Gregory Kavka, in his paper "Some Paradoxes of Deterrence,"[11] suggests that several genuine paradoxes emerge from special deterrent situations where forming the intention to retaliate against serious offenses might prevent great evil, but carrying out the act of retaliation would itself be morally wrong (as in the case of deliberately killing millions of innocent people in retaliating against evil leaders who perpetrate aggression). These paradoxes occur, according to Kavka, as a result of our acceptance of important moral principles which seem so obviously in accord with our moral intuitions. One of these "bridge principles" (so called because they relate our evaluations of actions to our evaluations of agents) is the following: "To intend to do what one knows to be wrong is itself wrong."[12] Thus, while the *intention* to retaliate in kind against a nuclear attack brings about a great deal of good in the world (Paskins and Dockrill had claimed this to be the guarantor of peace since 1945), the intention itself must be wrong since the *act intended* is wrong. If we assume that mere bluffing will be found out and hence for the deterrent to be effective we must genuinely intend to carry out nuclear retaliation, then the paradox seems inescapable. Forming the intention is morally right (it prevents enormous harm), and forming the intention is morally wrong (if the act itself is wrong, then intending to do it is also wrong). A thorough discussion of this paradox would take us beyond the limited scope of this chapter and perhaps involve rigorous analysis of utilitarian versus deontological foundations of ethical principles. I mention it here for two reasons: first, to point up the moral complexity of the deterrence issue itself, and second, to relate that complexity to the discussion question before us.

Should we despairingly abandon our attempts to find a rational path through the moral difficulties generated by the current state of modern warfare and simply "rely on God for our protection"? This would seem to me to abdicate the responsibility of our stewardship for the world, a stewardship which we find implicit in the views of the medieval Christian thinkers who attempted to synthesize the spiritual and material aspects of human existence. When the gates to the Garden of Eden were closed on man, we were not promised a rose garden in which to work out our salvation but something quite different. God does not intervene frequently in human history. He has provided man with reason and grace, and these are the instruments we must rely upon in coping with the problems of defense against aggression.

Notes

1. Elizabeth Anscombe, "War and Murder," in *Nuclear Weapons: A Catholic Response*, edited by Walter Stein (Merlin Press Ltd.), 1961 and included in *War, Morality, and the Military Profession,* edited by M.M. Wakin (Boulder, Colo.: Westview Press), 1979, 285-298. My argument in this chapter against Christian pacifism is heavily influenced by Anscombe's discussion.

2. Anscombe, *War, Morality, and the Military Profession*, 293.

3. Anscombe, *War, Morality, and the Military Profession*, 286.

4. Louis Fischer, *Gandhi—His Life and Message for the World* (New York: New American Library [Mentor Edition], 1954).

5. Louis Fischer from *Gandhi* (note 4) as excerpted in *Bhagavad-Gita* (New York: New American Library [Mentor], 1951), 142

6. Anscombe, "War and Murder," in *War, Morality, and the Military Profession*, 286-287.

7. Lt. General Sir John Winthrop Hackett, "Today and Tomorrow," from his lectures entitled *The Profession of Arms*, as included in *War, Morality, and the Military Profession*, edited by M.M. Wakin, 91-105.

8. Hackett, "Today and Tomorrow," 93.

9. Morris Janowitz, *The Professional Soldier* (1960, 1970), see especially chapter 20.

10. Barrie Paskins and Michael Dockrill, *The Ethics of War* (Minneapolis: University of Minnesota Press, 1979).

11. Gregory S. Kavka, "Some Paradoxes of Deterrence," *The Journal of Philosophy*, 75 (June 1978) or reprinted in *War, Morality, and the Military Profession*, edited by M.M. Wakin, 505-525.

12. Gregory Kavka, "Some Paradoxes of Deterrence," 509. This principle is accepted literally by many of the great moral philosophers of the West, including several of the medieval Christian theologians.

Chapter 14

JUST WAR, NUCLEAR DETERRENCE, AND THE STRATEGIC DEFENSE INITIATIVE

We begin our reflections on these most difficult and sensitive problems by setting forth the moral premises relevant to any discussion of modern warfare.

My first premise is that one of the major purposes of government is to provide for the security of its people, and this purpose takes the form of a moral obligation which cannot be set aside without destroying the concept of the nation-state. There are many ways of defending the political sovereignty and territorial integrity of a nation, and one of these ways is the use of military force. Those who share responsibility for the public well-being may not abjure the use of force if it is necessary to defend the state against aggression; that is to say, public officials may not be pacifists as a matter of principle. This premise is supported by the U.S. Catholic Bishops in their pastoral letter, The *Challenge of Peace*, where they state:

> The council and the popes have stated clearly that governments threatened by armed, unjust aggression must defend their people. This includes defense by armed force if necessary as a last resort.

Second, I accept the most general principles of classical just-war theory which make it possible to distinguish the just use of military power from the unjust use of such power. The just use will include the traditional conditions of legitimate authority, just cause, right intention, right use of means, last resort, some fair chance of success, and proper proportionality. "Right use of means" will include the principles of discrimination and proportionality of the means used.

I think it follows from the acceptance of the conditions of just-war theory as well as from just plain common moral sense that a total war, a war in which there would be an all-out nuclear exchange, a war in which there would be no

---

Elements of this chapter have been presented at a number of conferences and as a lecture on a number of college campuses during the 1980s.

discrimination between combatant and noncombatant, a war which could result in the destruction of humanity, could never be viewed as a just war. It could not satisfy the conditions of right intention, proportionality, right use of means, etc. Moreover, such a result must be viewed by all rational agents as a great physical and moral evil. All of this may seem extremely obvious but from this simple reflection comes an important conclusion concerning the nature of *sane* military policy: we must *avoid* total war; we must in fact *prevent* total war. The function of the modern military then becomes what Morris Janowitz has called a *constabulary* function and General Hackett has characterized as the *containment of violence*. While total war must be avoided, it seems highly unlikely that warfare at some lesser level can be avoided (have there really been seventy different wars since the end of the last general war in 1945?), and hence we must do something about these wars to assure their limitation to the lowest level of violence possible; we must prevent their escalation to what we have called "total war."

There are many sophisticated analyses of the issues surrounding the use of nuclear weapons, especially as regards the moral paradoxes associated with their deterrent function. Sometimes it is easy to lose sight of what it is that is supposed to be *deterred* by a policy of nuclear deterrence. *Nuclear* deterrence is one of the ways we have adopted to attempt to prevent *total war*; it is very obvious that the existence of a nuclear deterrent has not prevented all levels of warfare between nation-states nor within nation-states.

We can at least ask ourselves, is nuclear deterrence the only effective way to prevent the use of nuclear weapons in a total war? But when we ask that question, we must be sure to do so in the context of the actual world situation we now find ourselves in, a situation that includes a very large number of nuclear warheads in the possession of several nations and in at least one of those nations many of those nuclear weapons are aimed at the United States and its NATO allies. In that realistic context is it reasonable to suppose that a nuclear balance is better calculated to deter total war than a nuclear imbalance? Where does sanity lie? Ideally, if we wish to remove the threat of a nuclear holocaust entirely, this can only happen if all nuclear weapons in existence are dismantled in parallel and simultaneous fashion. A nuclear freeze as proposed by many will not accomplish this task. A publicly announced "no first use" policy does not seem likely to bring this about either. Since the *knowledge* necessary for the production of nuclear weapons is not likely to disappear, perhaps their existence in several hands serves as deterrent to their use by any one possessor of them.

But what if we were to take the initiative and announce a unilateral freeze or go even further to a unilateral dismantling? If we were to do either of these actions unilaterally and if our doing so were to make our nation highly vulnerable to attack or to nuclear blackmail by other nuclear powers, then such moves might be considered an abdication of the moral obligation our public officials have to provide for our defense against potential external enemies.

So what morally acceptable options do we have with regard to our attempts to avoid total war? May we engage in a different moral analysis of nuclear weapons viewed as deterrent forces than of nuclear weapons viewed as actually used in an all-out war? Many of our best thinkers have already pointed out in agonized fashion the difficulties associated with such a task. But given the critical importance of avoiding total war can we shrink from the task of evaluating realistically the moral status of nuclear deterrence? If total war is a moral evil can its *prevention* by this means be simply dismissed as itself being innately evil?

Let me make at least one very simple, perhaps simple-minded, attempt to view nuclear deterrence as morally plausible until the time when through arms reduction negotiations nuclear weapons might be totally eliminated by all possessors. Many of our colleagues, including the U.S. Catholic bishops, have pointed out that if deterrence fails and we are faced with carrying out our threat to use nuclear weapons in retaliation, such use would be immoral since it would of necessity fail to discriminate between combatant and noncombatant, would perhaps kill millions of innocents and neutrals, and would hasten the destruction of all humanity. And—so the argument goes—if the actual use would be immoral, then the threat to use and forming the intention to use them must also be immoral. Some thinkers, Michael Novak for one, have argued that this is the wrong moral analysis. He suggests that the proper moral principle to apply is to "make the moral choice that occasions the fewest evil consequences" and that abandoning deterrence would be the greatest evil "for it entails endangering that liberty which is more precious than life itself." This argument in its barest form has been challenged because it seems to rest entirely on a judgment of consequences as do most moral judgments based on choosing the lesser evil. One might avoid this criticism if instead of merely weighing consequences, one views the deterrence issue as presenting us with a choice between conflicting moral obligations which cannot all be satisfied simultaneously. Our leaders are morally obliged to prevent Total War and in the present circumstances, nuclear deterrence is the most direct means available for fulfilling that obligation. But nuclear deterrence carries with it the threat to innocent life that if acted upon would be morally evil, and we are morally obliged to avoid the intentional destruction of innocent life. It is at least plausible to judge that in these circumstances the higher moral obligation is to take the action which deters total war even with the attendant risks that the deterrence would fail. Our hope, of course, is that the circumstances will change in the future so that this particular set of moral obligations will no longer be the only group of choices available.

Most arguments associated with the use of nuclear weapons, either as tactical counterforce-limited war-fighting weapons, or as strategic weapons, or as purely deterrent in nature, quickly move to a condemnation of all wars, even wars of self-defense. The reason this happens is that we seem only to concentrate on *how* wars may be fought, forgetting entirely the question of *whether* a nation may have the moral right or moral duty to fight, especially in self-defense. This argument seems to go as follows: if nuclear weapons are wrong to use, then wars in which they might be used must be morally condemned. This argument must be taken very seriously, but I have an uneasy feeling about it, and if I tell you why perhaps we will share that uneasiness.

Torturing prisoners of war is morally wrong and legally forbidden by international treaties, but we must predict that some enemies will do so since they have in the past, and we are obliged then to prepare our combat troops to cope with it. The same may be said of the use of poison gas or of terrorist attacks on noncombatants. What we do *not* conclude is that fighting in a war in which prisoners are tortured or poison gas is used, is morally wrong. In fact, we conclude that the nation against whom these tactics and weapons are used may have its case for fighting a war against an enemy of this sort morally strengthened. Perhaps what we need to conclude is that the country contemplating using nuclear weapons in a war (or torture, or poison gas, or terrorist tactics) must be morally condemned if *it initiates* such a war but not that fighting in such a war becomes morally objectionable for all participants. What we may wish to condemn is the intentional use of mass destruction weapons against noncombatants. That position is easy to accept (though not always easy to apply), but it does not follow from that principle that wars of self-defense in which such weapons are used (perhaps initially by only one side) are immoral wars from the point of view of all participants.

For the past 40 years we have relied on nuclear weapons to deter total war, while recognizing that such a deterrent cannot serve in the same fashion to restrain all war fighting. There may be an analogy here with our system of criminal law and its accompanying threat of punishments which may deter many would-be criminals but obviously not all, that is, the system of criminal law carries with it always some aspects of successful deterrence. The existing apparatus of nuclear deterrence does not provide a threat effective against warfare as such—we need but look around our world and its history since 1945 to verify that this is the case. But like the criminal law structure, perhaps nuclear deterrence functions to prevent total chaos by deterring what we fear most—a total war—while mandating that the function of military action in the professional sense is to contain outbreaks of violence at the lowest level possible and, in any event, at some level below the escalation to total mobilization.

I will leave further discussion of this level of the nuclear deterrence issue to our question-and-answer period, realizing that the issue is fraught with moral complexity and that we have yet to say much much more about threats, intentions, and last resorts.

The Strategic Defense Initiative has introduced a new dimension to the moral discussions of nuclear deterrence that has several puzzling aspects. Much of the discussion has centered not on a moral issue at all but on controversy over whether such a system could ever be effective and whether the research and development costs could ever be justified. I am not an expert on laser technology, and I am confused by the responses of those who claim knowledge in this field. The claims and counterclaims about the possibility of developing and deploying defensive systems in space which would be capable of destroying launched ballistic missiles are not reassuring. But from the point of view of just-war theory, one would think that there is an obvious moral advantage in the development of a defensive system.

Surely the problem with proper intentions disappears if the motive for developing this new technology is to provide a defense against nuclear armed missiles. Even if nuclear deterrence fails, these proposed defensive weapons pose no threat for noncombatants nor do we need to worry about accidental nuclear triggering from such weapons. Thus the just-war concerns regarding discrimination are not at issue nor are concerns for proper proportion. Additionally, some have argued that if some reasonable level of defense against ballistic missiles can be achieved, that should facilitate agreements to reduce nuclear arsenals. Nuclear deterrence by defensive systems would seem to be remarkably more desirable than nuclear deterrence by offensive weapons. A reasonably effective defensive system might well also remove concerns that some would cheat on any negotiated nuclear arms reduction.

One of the arguments given for maintaining large nuclear arsenals has been that there must be a sufficient number of weapons so well protected that any potential aggressor would be deterred by the knowledge that any first strike would be met by severe retaliation from surviving weapons. Advocates of strategic defense systems point out that it is morally preferable to deter a first strike or neutralize it than to retaliate or even to threaten retaliation with a massive nuclear response. The obvious hope of such advocates is that the existence of defensive weapons, perhaps even shared defensive weapons, will persuade all nuclear powers that it is no longer necessary to even possess nuclear weapons. Deterrence of nuclear war through a policy of mutual survival seems much more attractive from the moral point of view than deterrence through a policy of mutually assured destruction or a policy of counterforce strategy.

If a defensive system is morally superior as a deterrent to nuclear war then why has the Strategic Defense Initiative created so much controversy in the United States and why have the Soviets become so disturbed about this possibility? Some of the opposition arguments are well known. First of all, we would have to withdraw from the 1972 Anti-Ballistic Missile (ABM) Treaty or renegotiate it before we could deploy the strategic defense system. There is some evidence that the Soviets have already violated the ABM Treaty, but that, by itself, is not sufficient provocation for us to eschew our treaty obligations without renegotiation. Another argument suggests that progress in research on strategic defense would make the nuclear risks greater since the Russians could well view the deployment of such a system as protection for our own offensive nuclear weapons and would be tempted to launch a preemptive strike before a defensive system is fully deployed. Still others argue, not about the moral superiority, but about the high cost and projected overall effectiveness of particle beam or laser defensive weapons. Harold Brown, William J. Perry, and George W. Rathjens, among others, have suggested that even with superb technological advances such ABM devices could never be 100 percent effective and only a "perfect" defense can suffice against weapons with such vast destructive power. Perry argues that even an antiballistic missile system that achieved a miraculous 95 percent effectiveness would still permit 300 Soviet nuclear warheads to reach American cities in an all-out launch.

Speculation of this sort comes at a time when we really do not know whether the technology needed for a reasonably effective defense against ballistic missiles can be developed. Meanwhile, more nations are attempting to attain nuclear capability and more prophecies are being made about how soon some of those nuclear weapons will be going off. The possibilities suggested by the Strategic Defense Initiative seem to be the only breakthrough in years of attempts to control nuclear weapons. Given the moral superiority of defensive technology can we not conclude that researching the feasibility of this technology is morally permissible? If the technology holds out the only real possibility of ridding the world of nuclear weapons, perhaps we might wish to hold that such research is morally obligatory.

Chapter 15

APPLYING NUREMBERG PRINCIPLES TO LIMITED WAR

The Nuremberg Principles

Before asking how the Nuremberg principles might be applied to limited war, we should first attempt to be clear about the principles themselves. What are they? Were they new when espoused in 1945 and 1946? Were there some difficulties associated with these principles and the Nuremberg (and Tokyo) trials in which they received application?

For purposes of this discussion I will characterize the Nuremberg principles as incorporating fundamental responses to three types of "crimes" charged to the leadership of the Axis powers in World War II: crimes against peace, war crimes, and crimes against humanity. The "crimes against peace" charge relates to the fact that in Europe, the Germans under Hitler started the fighting and that the war was an aggressive war, that is, it did not occur as a response to a previous wrong initiated by Germany's neighbors whom they attacked. Thus, the Germans violated the Kellogg-Briand Treaty of 1928, which outlawed wars of aggression and restricted "justified" wars to a single "just cause" namely, as responses to aggression (self defense). From this perspective the notion of "crimes against peace" is not new with the Nuremberg Trials—it was already accounted for in the Kellogg-Briand Treaty and even more broadly in the classical just-war principles of just cause and right intention which aggressive war clearly violates. However, what seemed new at Nuremberg was that *individuals* were held responsible for launching and waging aggressive war and were tried, convicted, and sentenced by an international court. Thus we may form Nuremberg Principle #1 as follows: *The waging of aggressive war is a personal and punishable crime.* Central to this first principle and indeed to any of the others we refer to as "Nuremberg Principles" is the strong emphasis on individual accountability. As Telford Taylor put it, "there are some universal standards of human behavior that laws transcend the duty of obedience to national laws" and, quoting a 1970 newsletter, "a citizen must *not* go along with policies he believes to be wrong."[1]

This chapter was initially prepared for a conference at Notre Dame University and delivered there in 1990. It has been accepted as a chapter in *Morals and Might: Ethics and the Use of Force in Modern International Affairs*, to be published by Westview Press as edited by George Lopez and Drew Christiansen. Reprinted with permission.

The second of the Nuremberg principles, which also focuses on individual accountability, has to do with violations of the "law of war" as incorporated in the common law of nations, the many international treaties formulated at the various Hague and Geneva conventions, and the laws of warfare published by individual nations (in the United States, dating back to the Lieber Rules of 1863 and updated continuously in Department of Defense publications). Violations of these laws are frequently referred to as "war crimes," but the treaties and national laws do not provide the machinery for enforcement nor are there any specified penalties for war crimes. Prior to 1945, nations court-martialed their own military men who violated the laws of war; what was new at the Nuremberg and Tokyo trials was that an *international* tribunal undertook the trials and punishments of war criminals. What became explicit at these trials (although already part of the codes of several countries) was that the claim of obedience to superior orders was not in itself a sufficient defense for committing acts forbidden by the laws of war. Nazi and Japanese leaders, both military and civilian, were held responsible for criminal acts of their subordinates even when the leaders did not order the atrocities committed by their soldiers (as in the well-known case of the Japanese General Yamashita). We might formulate Nuremberg Principle #2 dealing with the war crimes issue in the following fashion: *Individuals who violate the laws of warfare may be held criminally liable in international courts and the plea of following superior orders is not an adequate defense when the orders are clearly unlawful.*

The "crimes against humanity" charge was leveled against the Nazi leaders who ordered and implemented the policy of arresting millions of persons not implicated in the armed struggle at all but who were "non-Aryans," particularly those of Jewish ancestry. The arrest, imprisonment in concentration camps under inhumane conditions, forced slave labor, medical experimentation, and finally wholesale destruction of these persons (at least six million of them) constituted such an abominable horror in its violation of human rights that there need not have been any specific laws prohibiting such actions, their moral wrongness being so frighteningly obvious. Those accused of these sorts of crimes also invoked a plea of "superior orders" but were, as in the case of the war crimes issues, held personally responsible when it was clearly established that they could reasonably be expected to know that those orders were immoral or unlawful. Nuremberg Principle #3 is difficult to formulate. The most obvious formulation is that: *Genocide against one's own citizens or against those of other nations is a personal and punishable crime.* This is the common approach but does not clearly include the condemnation of imprisonment of the innocent, slave labor, or experimentation on human subjects which ought to be part of this principle dealing with crimes against humanity. Another candidate for this formulation might be: *Wholesale violation of the human rights of one's own citizens or those of other nations is a personal and punishable crime.*

Difficulties with the Principles

I have already noted that the concepts incorporated in these Nuremberg principles are not new and were not new in 1945. The international tribunals were unusual, however, and the trials were not without their critics. The emphasis on individual responsibility was questioned by those who remained convinced that individuals ought not to be held responsible for "crimes of state." While aggressive war had frequently been condemned in the past, trials and legal punishments for this "crime against peace" were not previously conducted by international courts. The propriety of trying the "losers" in a tribunal made up of the "victors" was strenuously questioned: was the motive a genuine concern for justice or was it simple revenge? Serious claims were put forward that the Nuremberg Charter constituted *ex post facto* law. Further, the cooperation of the Russians with the Germans in partitioning Poland early in the war raised the issue of a nation trying others for crimes which it also committed. In spite of these objections the war crimes trials were conducted at Nuremberg, in Tokyo, and elsewhere and the phenomena known as the Nuremberg Principles have been added to the collection of common law, treaties, laws of warfare, and just-war theories all calculated to constrain man's inhumanity to man.

Influence of the Nuremberg Principles

In spite of the controversy associated with the trials held at the close of World War II, we can observe that the Nuremberg principles have had some significant influence although not on all nations and not in all conflicts. They have provided reinforcement to the Kellogg-Briand Treaty of 1928 through their incorporation in various United Nations declarations. Their focus on individual responsibility has had an influence on the educational process for future officers, at least in U.S. officer training programs. The issue of "superior orders" continues to receive significant attention in military court martials and in the literature of military ethics. The 1956 edition (still the current edition) of Army Field Manual 27-10, *The Law of Land Warfare*, devotes a chapter to "Remedies for Violation of International Law War Crimes" specifying that acting as a government official does not relieve responsibility for a war crime. It also specifies responsibility even when domestic law provides no penalty for a crime against international law. Provision 509 of Section IV (p. 182) seems to have caught the spirit of the Nuremberg principles in balanced fashion:

> The fact that the law of war has been violated pursuant to an order of a superior authority, whether military or civil, does not deprive the act in question of its character as a war crime, nor does it constitute a defense in the trial of an accused individual, unless he did not know and could not reasonably have been expected to know that the act ordered was unlawful. In all cases where the order is held not to constitute a defense to an allegation of war crime, the fact that the individual was acting pursuant to orders may be considered in mitigation of punishment.

The Nuremberg principles continue to provide an appeal for attention to genocide and other human rights violations. We should note, however, that this appeal was not strong enough to evoke United Nations (UN) action against the Khmer Rouge in Cambodia when they engaged in genocidal acts (perhaps caused the deaths of one and a half million of their own citizens) shortly after the withdrawal of U.S. troops from Vietnam. In spite of attempts by UN committees and others to come to grips with the issue of aggressive war, our world seems no closer than we have ever been to arriving at a consensus on what constitutes aggression. Certainly, neither the Nuremberg principles nor any other sets of laws or moral restraints have prevented nations or smaller subgroups from using military force to attempt to resolve differences.

In future wars may we expect the convening of international courts to try individuals for violating the Nuremberg principles? It seems highly unlikely that this will happen unless some events as cataclysmic as the Nazi crimes against humanity occur and the nations who generate these events are as totally defeated as were the Axis powers in World War II. The Nuremberg principles, however, are part of the large body of traditional moral and legal constraints applied to the uses of military force. Perhaps we can reflect beneficially on how, in normative fashion, these principles may be applied to limited wars.

Applications to Limited Wars

Often the distinction between total war and limited war is made on the basis of mobilization, i.e., are whole societies involved in the process of war fighting, are all of a nation's manpower and material resources mobilized for war, are many of the world's nations forced to choose sides, and are all the available weapons of devastation being employed. With these kinds of criteria, World Wars I and II are judged to be total wars. It seems clear that because of the technological developments since 1945, total war could not now satisfy the just-war conditions of proper proportion and right use of means. If we add to the above criteria, the additional explicit identifying characteristic that total wars are wars in which no distinction is made between noncombatant and combatant, between the innocent and noninnocent, then the case for rejecting such wars as both irrational and immoral becomes even stronger. Limited wars, on the other hand, involve the use of military force to achieve limited political objectives and are restrained in the use of means at some level deemed adequate to achieve the political end but always below the level of nuclear holocaust. Thus limited wars are conceived of as having both limited ends and constrained means and for just-war theorists this type of war may sometimes be morally justified.

In 1960, Morris Janowitz referred to the uses of military force in limited wars as a "constabulary function,"[2] predicting that such uses would become the norm in the future. The Korean and Vietnam Wars, the use of the Navy in the Persian Gulf, the interventions in Grenada and Panama all seem to approximate the role of a constabulary force which Janowitz described as a force "continuously prepared to act, committed to the minimum use of force, and seeks viable international relations, rather than victory, because it has incorporated a protective military posture."[3] All three of the Nuremberg principles can be viewed as consistent with the constabulary conception of military forces provided that the political objective sought is truly constabulary and not an act of aggression (much room for interpretation here), the means used are consistent with the laws of war, and the action is not aimed at harming the innocent.

The charges brought by the Nuremberg Tribunal (crimes against peace, war crimes, and crimes against humanity) were aimed at actions done under the guise of legitimate warfare but which were literally criminal actions not entitled to whatever moral or legal status is bestowed on acts of war. Nuremberg Principle #1 clearly assumes the just-war conditions of "just cause" and "right intention" and proceeds to hold accountable those individuals who violate these conditions by initiating aggressive war. As already indicated, it has been impossible to achieve consensus on what precisely constitutes aggression although most commentators and statesmen seem to believe they can recognize it when they see it. I wish to maintain that striking the first blow is not always a clear indication that the side who strikes it is waging aggressive war. In instances where some grievous prior wrong has occurred or is in progress (Nation A is performing genocide against all of its citizens over age forty, for example), then if Nation B or Nations B and C should intervene with military force, we should not accuse B and C of violating the Nuremberg principle which prohibits aggressive war, even though they strike the first blow. In this case B and C can claim that they are responding to a prior wrong action by A, and indeed they may claim that A precipitated their response by violating Nuremberg Principle #3 that prohibits genocide.

It is most likely that Nuremberg Principle #1 will continue to serve as an additional support for the Kellogg-Briand Treaty but it is unlikely that it will serve as more than an ideal moral admonition. Even if it is violated, it is unlikely that legal punishment will occur except in extraordinary circumstances parallel to those already mentioned. Nuremberg Principle #2, which holds individuals responsible for war crimes even when following superior orders, has in fact been influential on the national level and should continue to function in this fashion. It clearly influenced the rewriting of national laws governing military conduct in the United States, Great Britain, and other countries, and those rewritten laws have been applied in military court-martials. It is unlikely, however, that international tribunals will be convened to try war criminals in the case of limited wars in the absence of the kinds of large-scale, horrible events that took place in World War II. The court-martials conducted in conjunction with the My Lai tragedy, while not sufficiently extensive, are examples of applications of Principle #2 on the national level and are typical of what may be expected in future wars. Individuals were held responsible for atrocities, were tried, some convicted—and all by their own country. In general, in the area of war crimes, Nuremberg Principle #2 continues to be effective in heightening concerns (at least in the U.S. military) for lawfulness and the moral legitimacy of military orders.

The Yamashita decision, rendered by a U.S. military commission in December 1945 condemned the senior Japanese commander in the Philippines for failing to control the Japanese troops who committed horrible atrocities against both military and civilians. General MacArthur confirmed the execution sentence for General Yamashita, but there has been considerable controversy concerning the principle involved. That principle seems to be that a commander is held responsible for crimes committed by his forces even if he did not order those actions and even if they were performed against his orders. Notice that this principle has not found its way into the list of Nuremberg principles and has rarely been applied (except in considerably altered form) since the Yamashita execution. Fairness seems to demand that we hold commanders responsible for crimes committed under their orders or even responsible for failure to issue appropriate restraining orders and instructions to their troops. Where it is doubtful that commanders could have controlled the actions of their troops, fairness restricts the amount of responsibility attributed to commanders. The general concern at Nuremberg for holding the actual perpetrators and those who ordered the crimes responsible would seem to protect commanders from prosecution if they had done neither. That same guidance serves as a severe constraint in attempts to discover appropriate responses to terrorism. Terrorist acts are generally crimes, not legitimate acts of war, and responses to terrorism must be directed against the perpetrators and those who ordered the criminal acts.

The most complex difficulties in applying the Nuremberg principles to limited war occur when we attempt to employ Principles #1 and #2 to evaluate guerrilla warfare, civil wars, and insurgencies. Where crowded theaters, school buses filled with children, teachers, and members of the clergy are targeted by guerrilla fighters or anyone else, and when such attackers are praised for destroying the "enemy," one is tempted to despair entirely of constraining such brutality. Indeed, in such circumstances, we are driven to conclude that because the distinction between the innocent and noninnocent is not maintained, this can no longer be described as limited war. Civilized nations will continue to insist upon observation of the law of war, buttressed by the Nuremberg principles even in these circumstances.

Notes

1. Telford Taylor, *Nuremberg and Vietnam: An American Tragedy* (New York: Bantam Books with the New York Times Co., 1970), 16.
2. Morris Janowitz, *The Professional Soldier* (New York: The Free Press, 1960), 418ff.
3. Janowitz, *The Professional Soldier*, 418.

Annotated Bibliography

Baird, Jay W., ed., *From Nuremberg to My Lai*, D.C. Heath and Co., Lexington, MA, 1972.

This volume contains an excellent introduction by the editor summarizing the results and debate surrounding the Nuremberg trials. It contains an excellent review of "The Law of the Nuremberg Trial" by Quincy Wright, the opening statement of Justice Robert H. Jackson, text of statements for the defense, commentaries concerning the legitimacy of the trials and their significance, special reviews of the Yamashita and Eichmann cases, and several materials attempting to relate the Nuremberg principles to Vietnam.

Department of the Army Field Manual 27-10, *The Law of Land Warfare*, July 1956, U.S. Government Printing Office.

This manual summarizes principal provisions of a number of treaties and Hague and Geneva conventions plus customary law governing the conduct of warfare. It is binding both upon states and individuals.

Hackett, General Sir John Winthrop, "The Military in the Service of the State" in Wakin, M.M., ed., *War, Morality, and the Military Profession*, Westview Press, Boulder, Colo., 1986, pp. 104-120.

General Hackett indicates we are living in a more Clausewitzian era when war and peace coexist; the period of crusades is over. He maintains that total wars must never be permitted but that we can expect limited wars to occur. He emphasizes the moral constraints on modern military forces and the virtues essential to the functioning of military professionals.

Janowitz, Morris, *The Professional Soldier*, The Free Press, New York,1960.

This study of the sociology of the U.S. military profession was long viewed as a classic but seems to have become neglected in recent years. Chapter 20, "The Future of the Military Profession" is of special interest to this topic since it realistically views the limited functions of the military (Janowitz calls it "constabulary") in the era of limited wars.

Taylor, Telford, *Nuremberg and Vietnam: An American Tragedy*, The New York Times Publishing Co., Bantam Book edition, New York, 1970.

This is probably the single most useful source on the issues of war crimes, superior orders, the Nuremberg legal principles, aggressive war, and individual accountability in war. Like the Baird volume listed earlier, it was compiled during the Vietnam War.

Chapter 16

HUMANITARIAN INTERVENTION: AN IDEA WHOSE TIME HAS COME

In his 1960 classic, *The Professional Soldier*, Morris Janowitz described the function of the American military as that of a "constabulary force" which is "continuously prepared to act, committed to the minimum use of force, and seeks viable international relations, rather than victory." Recent uses of the U.S. military seem to be consistent with Janowitz's characterization. Military intervention for limited political objectives departs from pre-1945 prescriptions for the U.S. military which was frequently viewed as embarked on all-out crusades to "make the world safe for democracy" or "fighting the war to end all wars." Total war in an age of nuclear weapons is neither practical nor moral. Limited war or "low intensity conflict" has become commonplace. What conditions can morally justify military intervention under the "constabulary" concept?

Our first concern should be with the sovereignty of nation-states. Just as individual human beings, if they are viewed as having any rights at all, have a right not to be harmed or interfered with, so too, sovereign nations can be viewed as having a right of noninterference. The moral permissibility of intervention against this right of noninterference of individuals and nation-states is contingent upon the conduct of both. The normal state of affairs requires nonintervention (if there is a right, there must be a corresponding obligation not to interfere with that right). Individuals lose their right of noninterference when by their own actions they violate the rights of others. When someone attacks me with an obvious intent to harm, I am morally permitted to protect myself, even if that requires the use of violent force. If I am a parent and someone viciously attacks one of my children, then I am not only morally permitted to protect my children, I am very likely morally *obliged* to do so.

In similar fashion, it seems clear that those who have the care and responsibility of an entire community must take seriously the obligation to protect their community when it is threatened by aggression. Extreme pacifism is not a reasonable option for those charged with the responsibilities of government. Thus, just-war theorists have maintained for centuries that when the last

This chapter was written for the Catholic News Service series called "Viewpoints" and was published in a number of the newspapers they serviced in February 1993. Reprinted with permission.

resort to peaceful means of resisting aggression has been exhausted, the legitimate authority in a society may declare war where the cause is clearly just, intentions are morally consistent with that just cause, and the means employed are properly proportional and discriminate between the innocent and the non-innocent. Direct aggression against the sovereignty of a nation then may sometimes be resisted by military force and it is sometimes morally obligatory to resist such aggression when the just-war conditions are satisfied. These considerations are the same ones to be applied when we turn to the issue of the use of military force in humanitarian interventions.

When one nation violates the sovereign rights of another nation and/or the human rights of its citizens, and the victim nation lacks sufficient means to resist, that cannot be a matter of moral indifference to the other nations of the world. If other nations are bound to the victim nation by a mutual defense treaty, that treaty may provide the moral permissibility of intervention. If no treaty connection exists, it may still be the case that the obligation not to intervene against the aggressor is overridden by the obligation to protect the innocent—the relative strength of that overriding obligation determines whether intervening is merely permissible or obligatory.

When Iraq violated the sovereignty of Kuwait and the human rights of Kuwait's inhabitants, it made itself vulnerable to response from other nations which could not avoid their responsibilities toward the victims of aggression. In this case, the intervention in constabulary fashion by the coalition states of the United Nations seemed justified in the face of the violations of the rights of person and property of the Kuwaitis. When an internal power like the Khmer Rouge in Cambodia visited genocide against its own people in the mid-1970s, that also should not have been a matter of moral indifference to the family of nations. There, humanitarian intervention would seem to have been morally justified and perhaps would have taken place had the tragedy not occurred at that point in history when the agonizing events in nearby Vietnam were reaching denouement.

The current military intervention in Somalia seems also to meet the test of just-war evaluation. Under anarchical conditions the nonmilitary humanitarian aid to starving inhabitants turned out to be totally ineffective. Whatever sovereignty rights might have existed for Somalia could scarcely be identified with any legitimate governmental structure in the winter of 1992-1993. Here the obligation of other nations equipped to feed and manage the distribution of aid to thousands of starving, disease-ridden human beings seems so clearly binding that it needs no sophisticated justification. The fact that rescue could be effected only by armed forces against armed criminal bands made the use of constabulary military force by the rescuing forces permissible and perhaps even obligatory.

The use of military force even in humanitarian interventions is not always justified. Concern must always be given to the sovereign rights of nation-states, but where important human rights are being violated, where nonmilitary means are ineffective, then, as a last resort, when relevant just-war considerations are satisfied, the use of military force by rescuing nations is morally permissible and sometimes morally obligatory.

Part V

DO WE KNOW WHAT WE'RE DOING?

Chapter 17

MILITARY AND SOCIETAL VALUES: THE RELEVANCE OF KNOWING AND DOING

I

Many years ago when I learned I was going to have the opportunity to study philosophy at the graduate level, I was tremendously excited. What a wonderful opportunity this would be, I thought, to sit at the feet of Socrates and be enlightened by those who studied the crucial problems of human existence. I expected that senior philosophy professors would be marvelous role models in their personal lives and I looked forward with great anticipation to associating with those who had solved the problems of the universe.

Indeed, these senior professors seemed very wise. They were dazzling in their abilities to rattle off the names and theories of great thinkers from every era. They knew the views of those whose names I couldn't even pronounce and I said to myself. "I'll never be able to grasp all of these ideas nor remember them well enough to teach them to others." But as time went on, I was slightly devastated to observe that these senior professors were not, as a group, the congenial masters of everyday living I expected them to be. They were not all basically *kind* persons—not even to each other. In fact, some would occasionally cross the street to avoid meeting and speaking with a colleague. And some had difficulties in their most important personal relationships—divorce, legal squabbles, envy, character assassination, narcissism—hardly what I had hoped for in the most knowledgeable, most studious persons in our society.

Was Plato wrong then, when he insisted that *knowledge is virtue*? Does a similar disillusion infect us all when we see the members of our public professions dissemble? When those highly educated attorneys in our society, those most knowledgeable about the law, find ways to use technicalities in that law to frustrate justice, do they not foster a moral cynicism among the rest of us? When politicians abuse power and position, when physicians prescribe unnecessary surgery, when the clergy substitute circus for spiritual sincerity, when military leaders lie under oath to their own citizens—what does the ordinary person conclude?

This paper was delivered in January 1995 at the National Defense University in Washington, D.C., for the Joint Services Conference on Professional Ethics (JSCOPE).

Clearly we have learned that there is a significant difference between *knowing* and *doing*. And we must be very careful how we interpret this difference lest we fall into the convenient traps of moral nihilism or moral relativism. Of course the highly educated members of our public professions *know* that kindness and courtesy and honesty and justice are virtues important to the success and survival of any society. But *knowing* this and *acting* in accordance with this knowledge may be two different things. While wisdom is itself one of the important virtues, it does not seem to guarantee the practice of the *moral* virtues. Knowledge is surely *necessary* for the development of virtue but it is not *sufficient*.

Now, how is this rather abstract reflection relevant to the issue at hand, namely, the relationship between military and societal value systems? Some might say there is a clue in the oath of office taken by every member of our military profession. All commit themselves to both support and defend the U.S. Constitution as a condition of military service. Many believe that the basis for our societal value system is contained in that Constitution which spells out fundamental rights and freedoms. Essentially, those values specifically mentioned in the Constitution characterize a way of life which respects human dignity—protected individual rights within the context of a pluralistic community. The military profession in this country is charged with the preservation and protection of that way of life—consistency would seem to demand that military members themselves exemplify in their personal lives those values to which they have made a clear and overt commitment. Does this mean that military and societal values are the same? Does this mean that if military people have *knowledge* of the values and corresponding virtues to which they are committed, they will *act* virtuously? Let's consider.

II

If we ask the empirical question, "What is the status of societal values in U.S. society today?" we are likely to find confusing answers. Contemporary crime statistics are discouraging, both from the numbers and types of crimes being committed. If we turn to the media we discover that according to opinion polls, many Americans admit to doing and tolerating dishonest action (cheating in school, cheating employers, stealing, cheating on taxes, etc.). If contemporary movies and TV depict and influence our behavior, we might conclude from them that infidelity, insincerity, adultery, envy, drug use, selfishness, and material acquisitions are commonplace and desirable as lifestyles or values. Our empirical sources of societal values seem to emphasize the sensational and the sordid. Pressure from these sources is felt mostly by the young (both in age and in moral maturity). It is sometimes difficult for the immature to avoid the message that this is what people are doing, so it must be okay.

But what does our society know about moral values? From our Constitution, from human history, from our churches and homes and teachers (sometimes) and our reasoning abilities and experience we have acquired over thousands of years some basic *knowledge* about moral conduct. We know that honesty is better than dishonesty, that courage is better than cowardice, that truth-telling is better than lying, that promise-keeping is better than promise-breaking, that humane treatment is better than torture, that protecting the innocent is better than intentionally harming them, that justice is better than injustice, that respecting human dignity is better than destroying it, that human freedom is better than slavery, that goodwill is better than envy, that courtesy is better than rudeness, that respect for others' property is better than theft or destruction, and essentially that there is a fundamental difference between right and wrong human conduct. We know these things and they are easy to express in general terms apart from the infrequent specific circumstances in which they may seem to conflict and require resolution.

Now, which are our societal values in the United States? Do we value truth and justice and courage and honesty or do we value selfishness, acquisitiveness, and infidelity? Notice that the sources of these sets of values differ. We know that honesty is better than dishonesty, and we do not openly teach the immature that dishonesty is morally right. But depicting dishonest lifestyles in an almost approving manner may influence the conduct of the immature more than the value *knowledge* we have and are sometimes fearful to teach. We know what we *ought* to do but we do not always do it. Some may wish to conclude that we value *all* of those virtues and vices already mentioned because we are such a pluralistic society. I cannot accept this as a satisfactory answer since reason and experience and human history, plus a decent smattering of common sense, all loudly proclaim that dishonesty, falsehood, drug addiction, infidelity, selfishness, and a host of other values we once labeled as vices, if universally practiced, can destroy all the conditions of existence that make human dignity possible. If, as a matter of fact, we *do* value all of these virtues and vices, then it becomes extremely difficult to be hopeful about our future as a society.

III

In his classic 1957 study, *The Soldier and the State*, Samuel Huntington points out that the American military became professionalized when it was most isolated from the mainstream of American society and its basically liberal value system. He describes the professional military ethic as a form of "conservative realism" which is considerably different from American liberalism but nevertheless compatible with the U.S. Constitution, which he views as a fundamentally conservative document. Huntington describes various periods in the history of the American military when it attempted to become more involved in the mainstream of politics and business but quickly returned to its isolation and more conservative value system. American society generally fosters individualism and the freedoms and rights of the individual. The military profession generally fosters conformity, obedience, hierarchical organization, and subordination of the individual to the unit. The military values unit and mission loyalty which can often be in conflict with extreme individualism. For Huntington, the military's isolation from civilian values seemed to guarantee its professionalism; its pessimistic view of human nature guaranteed its readiness to respond to national emergencies—its preparedness to fight.

In 1960 and again in 1970, Morris Janowitz (*The Professional Soldier*), observed that the American military had in fact, after World War II, become less alienated from American society and was indeed adapting to civilian values. He did not see that as necessarily diminishing military professionalism and indeed saw a need for more understanding of international politics and more interaction between the military and civil society. General Sir John Winthrop Hackett, in his modern day observations of the military and civilian society, also comments on their merging both socially and in their skills. But all three of these scholars of the military profession rightly perceive that the uniqueness of the military function will always keep its leading practitioners slightly apart from the mainstream of civilian society and certain societal values.

Where do military and civilian values converge and where must they diverge? It seems that healthy convergence flows from those virtues and values mentioned earlier as elements of human knowledge confirmed by reason, experience, and human history. The elemental human rights mentioned in the U.S. Constitution comprise an abbreviated listing of values critical to the way of life worth defending. Military professionals swear an oath to defend those values, that life style which incorporates the minimal conditions of human dignity. These values must be shared by military and civilian alike. Military professionals, however, in order to perfect the instrument of defending these values, of necessity curb their own exercise of some of these freedoms. They accept restrictions on the liberty to speak, they refrain from partisan politics, they are denied political office while on active duty, they accept restrictions on their freedom of movement, and in general subordinate personal preferences to the good of the military unit and the good of the country. In these ways, military values differ from civilian values—in ways involving the exercise of certain freedoms to act. Notice that the oath taken by military professionals constitutes a serious promise, and recall that we pointed out earlier that we know that promise-keeping is better than promise-breaking.

Obedience is an important military virtue because it is intrinsic to the military function. Obviously it is not an absolute; there are times when bad orders must be disobeyed. But in general, obedience is crucial in carrying out any ordered activity and in a military crisis it will spell the difference between success and failure. Notice that obedience is an important virtue in many areas of civilian society although its absence in civilian enterprises is rarely as catastrophic as in the military environment. When schoolchildren are undisciplined and disobedient in the civilian classroom, chaos results, education is diminished, and bad habits are learned but the immediate survival of the nation-state can hardly be viewed as at risk. Loyalty or fidelity to military mission, unit, and country are crucial to the fulfillment of the military function but infidelity to spouses in ordinary life often simply leads to divorce, not national disaster. Dishonesty in reporting the readiness of a military unit for battle could lead to national disaster while dishonesty in reporting the financial status of a corporation might merely lead to a business failure. A lack of courage in handling a domestic crisis might lead to individual harm—a lack of courage in carrying out the military function might lead to the loss of a battle and a country (way of life).

It seems clear that certain values and virtues are held to be important in both our civilian society and the military profession. Some values receive more attention and emphasis in civilian society (for example, personal freedoms) and some in the military profession (for example, obedience, loyalty, and courage). But having noted this, perhaps we should return to reflecting on the difference between knowing and doing, between knowledge and virtue.

Knowing that certain virtues are so essential to the military function that it cannot be accomplished without them is not the same as inculcating those virtues in military professionals. Knowing that respect for human dignity is essential to the success of the democratic society is no guarantee that people will respect those around them. Our knowledge of right and wrong does not come from merely observing current practice even though observing what others do does influence us. When we see many others looting during an urban riot, that may soothe our consciences if we decide to loot as well, but the fact that so many are doing it will not make looting morally right. For the military professional who observes false reporting becoming widespread among defense contractors there may be analogous temptations and rationalization of dishonest conduct but no amount of such conduct will make dishonesty morally right.

Military values and moral rules for military members can well be identical with societal values and moral rules so long as these fall into the category of the moral knowledge that is validated by human history, reason, and experience. Questionable moral practices, however, no matter how widespread they become should not become part of military practice (nor anyone else's) just because they are widespread. The question always must be, is this conduct morally right as tested against that fundamental moral knowledge already mentioned. What we *do* can only be morally correct when it conforms to what we *know* is morally right. If this formula is reversed, then the distinction between right and wrong conduct must inevitably disappear.

Military ethics is, like ethical standards for other professions, applied ethics. Applied ethics is a subset of ethics generally. Some ethical rules and moral values receive more emphasis in certain professions because of their unique services to society. Respect for patient autonomy (derived from respect for human dignity and the basic right not to be harmed) receives special attention in the medical profession. The obligation to obtain informed consent from competent patients is a very serious moral obligation for health care practitioners. Client confidentiality and serious efforts to obtain justice are special emphasis moral concerns for the legal profession. But all of these special obligations emanate from our more general moral principles regarding respect for human dignity, promise keeping, honesty, and our quest for a just society.

When doctors, lawyers, judges, clerics, teachers, government leaders, and military professionals fail to live up to our moral expectations (fail to *do* what we *know* is right) we feel cheated. When a society provides the professions with opportunities for education and training, and when the authority to act on our behalf has been bestowed, and when human life, justice, the national treasury, or the existence of the nation-state itself are at stake, then we expect our professionals to exhibit the best of the relevant moral virtues. When they substitute personal gain for societal service, when they harm patients or clients, when they behave in incompetent or immoral ways, then we react with moral outrage no matter what the popular practices in society generally might be at the time. When members of these public professions truly exemplify moral virtue through what they *do* in accordance with what we all *know* to be right, they can have an enormous positive moral influence on society.

Strange as it may sound, a competent military profession whose practitioners are characterized by loyalty, obedience, courage, integrity, and selflessness can be a moral anchor for a parent society that sometimes founders on huge waves of moral relativism, egoism, and acquisitiveness. In a 1990 Gallup Poll, 68 percent of Americans responded to the question "Who do you trust?" by expressing confidence in the military. No other U.S. institution (newspapers, banks, congress, religions) came close to that percentage. I wonder why.

Chapter 18

TECHNOLOGY AND EDUCATION: A PHILOSOPHER'S PERSPECTIVE

"Without a firm idea of himself and the purpose of his life, man cannot live and would sooner destroy himself than remain on earth, even if he was surrounded by bread."

(Dostoevski's Grand Inquisitor)

I would like to use this quotation from Dostoevski's "Grand Inquisitor" as the theme for the thoughts I'd like to share with you this afternoon concerning technology and education. A little over a month ago, at a Hertz Foundation Directors' Dinner, Edward Teller commented on what applied science and technology had accomplished during the war in the Persian Gulf, or "Desert Storm." He asserted that the United States Air Force had won that war single-handedly, in record time, with almost no casualties. He attributed this remarkable accomplishment to our astonishing developments in technology, while at the same time he lamented the fact that our society in general does not appreciate technology, is not comfortable with technology, and in large part lives in *fear* of technology. Is there a story here to be told which may help us to understand our love-hate relationship with technology?

Once upon a time, in the sixth century B.C. in ancient Greece, we felt the stirrings of what was to become known as "science" in the western world. Those early thinkers, referred to by historians of philosophy as the "pre-Socratics"—Thales and Anaximander and Empedocles and Heraclitus and Democritus—all seemingly sought to explain an assumed underlying unity in the physical universe. It is with that assumption, that there is order in nature to be discovered and explained, that science has its beginning. But material science as we know it was to remain in a dull and slumbering position for the next several centuries as Western thinkers turned full attention to the social and political issues which threatened the developing Greek and later Roman civilizations. Primitive (in modern eyes) technology responded to needs generated by agriculture and war, but natural science rested in the background, at best supporting the physics,

This paper was delivered as the principal talk at the May 1995 Outstanding Educator Colloquium at the United States Air Force Academy.

metaphysics, or moral philosophies of the great thinkers. We remember Epicurus and Lucretius as moral philosophers; the underpinning of atomic structure in nature which they provided for their moral theories is subsidiary.

Socrates, Plato, and Aristotle were most critically concerned about the nature of man, the nature of mind, how we acquire knowledge, the "laws" of thought, implications for moral conduct, and the best political structures for the kind of being man was thought to be. From these classical thinkers emerges a picture of humans as reasoning beings, responsible moral agents, capable of autonomous judgment and action. Persons emerge from these philosophies as potentially noble, creatures distinct in kind, function, and significantly higher in ultimate purpose than any of nature's other creatures. Humanity has dignity.

As theology moved into prominence in the Western intellectual world, and the early doctors of the Christian church adopted the classical Greek views of man's rational soul, Plato's conception of the supreme form of the good becomes identified with the Judeo-Christian view of a personal, creative God. By the Middle Ages, philosophy and theology were in the ascendancy. That is not surprising since they offered humans complete understanding and eternal happiness. There may be some truth in the observation that large numbers of Europeans were content to accept subservient life styles and minimal conditions of existence because of the hope held out for eternal felicity after death. Dostoevski may have been correct in agonizing over the role of man under the control of a church with political power—philosophers and theologians were not entirely successful in maintaining the Greek-inspired view of rational man as the foundation stone for political structures and legislation. The philosophers and theologians did not bring mankind total peace and happiness when they were in the dominant position. But today, science and technology are in the ascendancy and perhaps for much the same reason: they promise complete understanding and eternal happiness—now. Are we justified in transferring our full allegiance to them?

The Evils of Science and Technology

Science and technology represent knowledge and power. Advances in science are advances in human understanding of the physical universe; advances in technology herald advances in the conditions of human existence. Clearly these must be the highest source of goodness for man in the modern world and deserve our highest esteem and respect. And yet, we are besieged on all sides by criticisms of the evils and predicted evils of a civilization directed by technology. Earlier criticism came from the humanists who perceived that "science" had diminished human stature and had destroyed human dignity, which was so carefully established by the Greek, medieval, and Renaissance thinkers. Jacques Barzun recounts "the 'three great hurts' inflicted by science on the vanity of man: Copernicus (or Newton) displaced man from the center of the universe, Darwin thrust him back into the animal kingdom, and Freud put him at the mercy of his unconscious."[1] All three of these major scientific contributions were indeed viewed with suspicion by the ordinary person who followed the lead of the philosophers and theologians who resisted and challenged these advances.

Contemporary humanistic concerns deal more specifically with what is happening to persons as entire cultures are caught up in the sweep of technology. The catalogue of complaints is a long one: existence in a technological society has become sterile and artificial; imagination and creativity are stifled in favor of inexorable quantitative approaches to each social or political problem; education, wars, communications, even our approaches to recreation are dominated by technology; the environment is becoming polluted, nature desecrated in the name of technological progress. The blessings brought by science and technology are mixed: they have brought us better health and longer life—and an overpopulated planet; marvelous energy-consuming machines which ease the pains of human labor—and deplete the earth's sources of energy; better understanding of our biological makeup—and greater danger to human survival if wrong turns are taken in DNA research; more efficient and more powerful weapons to deter aggressors—and danger of total destruction of humanity; remarkable visual communications systems—and diminishing verbal skills; travel at incredible speeds—and inattention to where we are going.

Many humanists have pointed out that science and technology themselves are neither good nor evil but have the potential for either in the hands of scientists and technologists. The Reverend Theodore Hesburgh, in delivering a stirring commencement address at MIT several years ago, challenged the engineering graduates to concern themselves with the moral purposes to which they devoted their technological skills. In viewing the great problems of hunger, illiteracy, poverty, and disease around the world and the accompanying despair for millions of human beings he commented that:

> Against this background, I am slightly nauseated when I see science and technology dedicated to trivial purposes like better deodorants and better detergents, better cosmetics and more aesthetic telephones, better garden sprinklers and better remote control of wrestling and horse operas on television.[2]

Perhaps his most memorable remark highlighting his focus on appropriate purposes for technology was: "Personally, I am not interested in better dog food when people are hungry."[3]

Alexander Solzhenitsyn, in his highly publicized address at Harvard in 1978[4] sounded a similar theme, decrying the loss of man's spiritual life as his technological progress was concentrated almost entirely on physical well-being. He suggests that just as man's physical nature was neglected or even trampled by the theological views of the middle ages, his spiritual being has been neglected (even trampled) by the materialistic emphasis of modern technology.

And so the accusations against technology mount up. The critics say we have lost the essence of humanity in our mad rush to make the physical conditions of existence better, sometimes even seeming to prefer to play with technology's toys rather than direct ourselves to the physical needs of the underdeveloped nations or the nonphysical needs of persons. The current fascination with personal computers or the current fad of acquiring cellular phones are symbols of our concern with the quantitative and with gadgetry. The "quantitative attitude" is pervasive in our culture. Imagine judging a President's abilities or effectiveness by an almost daily index of his popularity as measured by Gallup, Harris, or NBC polls! Consider our great reliance on statistical data: the infamous body count in Vietnam as a measure of unit effectiveness, or the computerized hamlet evaluation system which purported to provide instant information on the status of pacification efforts in every hamlet in Vietnam. The emphasis on numbers, on sheer quantity as a measure of effectiveness, influences us in all areas of modern endeavor: How *many* units were produced this month compared to last month? How much more did this plant do than that plant? How many articles has this researcher or faculty member published this year? How many students are majoring in this discipline? One of the subtle results, over time, in our society of this emphasis on the quantitative is a loss of concern for the creative and the qualitative. "Things" don't last very long; sometimes one insightful article over a lifetime is a contribution worth more than a hundred mediocre publications; our quality as a *people* is slipping at the same time that we claim to be dedicated to something called "total quality."

How Did We Get Here?

How have we arrived at this state of affairs that sees so much of the blame for depersonalization, loss of human excellence, pollution of the environment, even moral indifference placed on the explosive advance of modern technology? Are we really doing worse for mankind with science and technology in the saddle than when philosophers and theologians held the reins of intellectual leadership? Perhaps a look at our attitudes toward the methods of physical and moral science will provide some explanatory background for these questions. The clear popular myth is that natural science is objective—it deals with facts, while moral philosophy is subjective—it deals with values. The early Greek emphasis on reason has found its modern home in mathematics and the scientific method. Reliable truth, objective truth, is to be found through the inductive-deductive process of the scientific method. Moral truths are perceived as not being nearly so reliable. It is not too great an exaggeration to refer to scientific results as public and verifiable while relegating moral valuations to the realm of "personal" feelings and preferences. Having done this, it is an easy move to render fact and value completely separate from each other and even easier to suggest that "real" truth is to be found only through the scientific method. Reason employed to produce moral insights, the emotional and intuitive life of the mind, even the imagination—these are no longer viewed as important in the lifestyle of modern persons.

Clearly, we are comfortable with the public nature of scientific truth. However remarkable scientific discoveries might be, it is reassuring to understand that the results are verifiable and that unfounded claims (e.g., "Piltdown Man") will be exposed by examination of the factual evidence. The power of scientific knowledge in the hands of the technician is daily demonstrated in our kitchen appliances, the remarkable advances in miniaturization, explorations of outer space, our engines of travel, our weapons of destruction, the communications superhighway, etc. It is easy to accept the popular myth that the physical sciences have progressed to the point where almost any truth about the universe of fact is accessible to man but that the moral philosophers have made no advances in understanding human values in the last 2,000 years.

This attitude takes peculiar turns, resulting in some amazing nonsense, a recent bit of which is delightfully demonstrated by an advertisement for itself in *Time* magazine. The ad features a portrait of Einstein and is captioned, "Everything is relative." It states that, "In the cool, beautiful language of mathematics, Einstein demonstrated that we live in a world of relative values."[5] Of course, Einstein did not demonstrate anything at all about "relative values;" his famous vision is about physical objects and their relations to each other. Both Einstein's theory and Heisenberg's indeterminancy principle have been used erroneously to support or destroy various positions on the status of moral principles and the questions of free will. The mere familiarity of their names is additional testimony of the ascendancy and the influence of science in our time.

From this reflection on the overwhelming appeal of scientific objectivity follows an observation worth considering. We want facts; we want, if possible, absolute certainty. Science and its natural applications through technology seem to provide exactly what we want. We may even have concluded quite literally that "science will save us." But the world of human decision-making is not that world of certainty—the actual world we operate in is rife with uncertainty precisely because human judgments frequently involve *valuing*, not merely describing.

Melvin Rader[6] provides a reasonable framework for distinguishing the functions of scientific, technological, and moral discourse which contains a special clue about the way we make evaluative judgments. He suggests that science *describes*: "This is a powerful herbicide." Alternatively, both technology and morality *evaluate*, but differently. Technology *evaluates hypothetically (prudentially):* "You ought to use a powerful herbicide" (if your task is to defoliate). Morality *evaluates normatively*: "You ought not engage in defoliation." The hypothetical or prudential "ought" of technology simply is an imperative of skill (in Kantian terminology); it tells how best to proceed to carry out our purposes. It does not, however, tell us what our purposes ought to be; technology's rules tell us *how* to carry out a task, not what our tasks ought to be. The latter is the function of morality, but the two are easily confused in a complex technological world. When former President Harry Truman explained that "having found the bomb, we have to use it,"[7] was he confusing the ought of technology with the ought of morality? In our classrooms at the Academy, are we careful to distinguish between these *prudential* oughts of technology and the *normative* oughts of morality?

With the view of science and technology as the saviors of mankind comes also the concomitant canonization of research. (The expression is Barzun's.) Research organizations occupy positions of great prominence in our society and are able to reach the purse strings of the university, the foundations, government, and industry much more easily than those who *do* or those who teach. The number of individuals and institutions devoted to doing research, directing research, recruiting for research, renewing funds for research, etc., is difficult to estimate, but it is very, very large. Barzun suggests that "Research… is no longer simply a vocation; it is an institution. One is tempted to call it the chief symptomatic institution of our scientific society after the obvious one of powerful machines."[8]

These remarks about research are not meant to be disparaging about the task and the need for scientific inquiry; it seems simply important to point up what a great change in our intellectual orientation has taken place because of the influential positions and the obvious successes of science and technology. It is revealing to realize that sometimes we provide funds for research institutions simply to keep them in operation, often only seeking to discover the specific problem being researched as a sort of afterthought. Let us turn now to what is clearly a value question, research for what? Is there some obligation to order priorities in research? Are some projects simply not worth doing? Can we really proceed in both science and technology as though the enterprises themselves are value free? Are the hundreds of thousands of papers being produced by U.S. faculty members being read by anyone, and how many of them are really worth reading?

As we noted in the previous reference to Father Hesburgh's commencement address at MIT, the decision about which human problems should benefit from our technological talent is itself an important moral decision. While it does not follow that if we spend as much money on researching heart disease or cancer as we do on weapons research that we will find "cures" or prevent them, nevertheless some priority for these health problems is morally relevant. Even if we can produce gasoline burning machines that will move faster than those now available, perhaps that technology is not worth doing if it will increase fuel consumption. Even if we can develop the technology to keep persons with nonfunctional organs alive indefinitely, should we devote our talents to this purpose? Just as there is perceptive moral concern to examine the possible side effects of new drugs before accepting them on the marketplace, so too, every scientist, every engineer, must accept the moral responsibility of reflecting on the moral worth of the next technological advance. We must constantly be sensitive to the distinction between the ought of technology (imperatives of prudence and skill) and the ought of morality, and give priority to the latter.

There is much in the literature on this subject, especially that written by "humanists," which places blame on the scientist and technologist for many modern ills, particularly the dehumanization of persons. The panacea recommended, of course, is to "humanize" the scientists and engineers by broadening their educational backgrounds—make them literate on the subject of human values. It would seem only fair to point out that many of those pointing the finger of blame are not "literate" in science and engineering—the humanists need also to broaden their educational backgrounds if only to help direct technology toward human good.

Conclusion

Against the background of these reflections it seems to me that the faculty of the Air Force Academy ought frequently to ask itself whether we are striking the right balance for *our* institution with regard to research and teaching. Do we have a balanced perspective also about technology's input on education: Are we spending inordinate amounts of time playing with computers or are we employing them properly as the helpful tools they ought to be? Are we spending more hours on the technology of our classroom preparations and projects than we are on the content of our teaching? Are the students the only ones who aren't doing enough reading of the material? Do we sometimes let technology dictate our pedagogy or do we put pedagogy first and then seek the assistance of technology?

Today we are honoring the *good* teachers. This should be a clear message to all that we care about teaching; that it is central to our concern as an institution, that in our order of priorities it comes first before research and first before technology. Most importantly perhaps, we may use this occasion to remind ourselves that although technology is in the driver's seat, it's only gear position is neutral—we and the cadets we teach must accept the responsibility for determining which gear is appropriate and which road is the morally right one to take.

Notes

1. Jacques Barzun, *Science: The Glorious Entertainment* (New York: Harper & Row, 1964), 62.

2. Theodore Hesburgh, "Science and Technology in Modern Perspective" (MIT, 1962) in *Thoughts for Our Times* (South Bend, Ind.: University of Notre Dame Press, 1963).

3. Hesburgh, "Science and Technology."

4. Published in the *National Review* under the title "A World Split Apart," July 7, 1978.

5. *Time*, September 24, 1979, 65.

6. Melvin Rader, *The Enduring Questions*, 3rd ed. (New York: Holt, Rinehart and Winston, 1976), 635ff. Rader's suggestions are a part of his commentary on a selection from John Dewey's *Ethics*.

7. Address to the Nation, August 9, 1945; quoted in R.A. Wasserstrom, *War and Morality* (1970), 83, and in R. Tucker, *The Just War* (1960), 21-22.

8. Barzun, *Science*, 122.

Part VI

AND IN THE END

Chapter 19

TEACHING PHILOSOPHY AT THE UNITED STATES AIR FORCE ACADEMY

"You don't want to teach philosophy to cadets at the Air Force Academy. You'll start them thinking!" So spoke my civilian philosophy colleagues in 1959 when I was en route to my teaching assignment at the Academy, fresh from completing a Ph.D. in philosophy, an eager first lieutenant, committed to this exciting new institution and its innovations in service academy education. My civilian colleagues, of course, were reflecting an outmoded stereotype of the professional military mind which I was (and am) totally determined to eradicate. Of course we want professional military leaders who are good thinkers; we not only went them, we require them! Dynamism and discipline *do* mix.

In those early years of the life of the Academy even our own colleagues and senior officers were a bit suspicious of philosophy. "What kind of philosophy are you teaching our cadets?" "Do we really need it in the curriculum?" "Are you an existentialist?" "What religion are you?" And we, too, who taught philosophy courses had our concerns. With only one core course, should we teach an introductory survey course? How much metaphysics and epistemology should future officers study? Shouldn't everyone take a basic course in logic? And what about moral philosophy? Doesn't every educated person need to be familiar with the works of Plato, Aristotle, Aquinas, Kant, Descartes, Hume, Mill, Marx, and other great thinkers? Should we read the original works or will secondary sources be better for cadets? Should we try to master theories of the great thinkers or concentrate on applying various concepts to the concrete problems of today and tomorrow? Can people with doctorates in English teach philosophy or must we send officers to earn graduate degrees in philosophy?

In seeking answers to these questions I've made a number of mistakes over the years. In my very first ethics course, we covered thirty-nine philosophers in one semester! My first logic course was absolutely too sterile, too mechanically formal, and not adequately applied. My first problems course was

---

This paper was prepared for a locally published journal dedicated to excellence in teaching at the Air Force Academy and was published in the winter of 1995.

wonderful for sophisticated Ph.D. candidates but probably rather mysterious for cadets in their very first philosophy course. But I think I did learn from those early teaching blunders as did we all—helping each other with both the subject matter decisions and our teaching styles. We learned that even when the topic of the day requires considerable lecturing, there is a difference between talking *to* your students and talking *with* your students. Successful teachers get every student involved even while delivering a lecture. We learned that the socratic dialogue can be really effective in explaining difficult concepts—if the teacher is sufficiently patient; if every student is drawn into the dialogue; if you spend your preparation time developing relevant, clear analogies and examples; if you never lose sight of the goal you wish the dialogue to achieve; if the students have been sufficiently motivated to read the material before the dialogue begins; and if you are convinced that mastering these concepts really *matters*.

The Vietnam War helped us make some decisions on core course choices and on the issue of theory versus application. When the Commander of Strategic Air Command called me to ask if it was possible (as two of our graduates claimed in their conscientious objector petitions) that one could study four years at the Air Force Academy and never discuss the morality of strategic bombing, I knew finally that if we only teach one core course in philosophy, it has to be an ethics course. Similar experiences and the testimony of POWs like Admiral Stockdale and Major General Borling (USAFA '63) helped with the issue of theory versus application—we had to do both. Yes—every educated military leader should know the difference between a strict consequentialist argument and a deontological argument and the difficulties with both positions. Yes—every military decision maker should be provided experience in making moral evaluations of specific cases and applications of just-war theory. Yes—every citizen in a democracy should be able to justify fundamental human rights and understand the source of our obligations to respect and defend them. Yes—every military planner, every battle leader, every would-be warrior must understand both the philosophical and practical justifications for the military virtues of loyalty, obedience, courage, integrity, and selflessness.

Sometimes as turf-protectors and teaching prima donnas we have gotten caught up in positions that have not benefited either our curriculum or our students. If I've learned anything about effective teaching these past thirty-six years, it's that we teach best when we help each other—when we teach together. If a brand new instructor (like I was in 1959) tries to teach undergraduates at the level of the graduate course she or he just completed, then experienced mentors ought to provide advice. If we share our successful analogies and examples; if we invite colleagues to observe teaching techniques that work; if we pool the marvelous competence, enthusiasm, and creative imagination this faculty brings to our classrooms, we can be the finest undergraduate teachers in this country. That is not where we are at the moment, but that is where we can be and where we ought to be.

I'll conclude these brief reflections by forcing myself to jot down those practices that I honestly believe make us better teachers.

1. Extensively prepare for each class on both the *material* to be covered during that class and the way in which it can be best taught (2 to 6 hours).

2. Know in advance what each cadet should without fail take away from *this* hour and summarize the key points in the last 5 minutes.

3. Exude *enthusiasm* for the ideas, skills, or information you're dealing with—every class.

4. Be *convinced* of the importance of this course you are teaching to the development of each student.

5. Be *sincere* in your commitment to this course and to the Academy mission.

6. Resolve to get every student *actively* involved every hour.

7. Constantly search for ways to help students accept *responsibility* for their own education.

8. Be *gracious* in *recognizing* and congratulating good thinking; be *firm* but *never sarcastic* in recognizing and rejecting nonsense.

9. *Visit* classes of your colleagues, both in your own discipline and in other disciplines. We have *much* to learn from each other.

10. Employ your *imagination* when teaching complex concepts or skills.

11. *Stop* at least once a week and ask yourself if you're achieving *satisfaction* from your teaching. If you're not finding it meaningful, the chances are that your students aren't either.

12. Reject the overwhelming *cynicism* that often invades academia. It is neither sophisticated nor healthy. Remain steadfast in your commitment to the possibilities of *human decency* and the importance of *ideas*.

ABOUT THE AUTHOR

Malham M. Wakin is Emeritus Professor of Philosophy at the United States Air Force Academy in Colorado Springs, Colorado. He has taught at the Air Force Academy since 1959 and served as Professor and Head of the Department of Philosophy, Chairman of the Humanities Division, Assistant Dean, Associate Dean, chair and member of numerous committees. He served on active duty with the Air Force from 1953 to 1995, including early tours as an Air Rescue navigator and a combat tour in Vietnam in 1968. He holds a number of military decorations including the Distinguished Service Medal and the Legion of Merit (three). He has authored or edited four other books, the best known being *War, Morality, and the Military Profession*. He has published many articles in a number of scholarly journals, mostly dealing with ethics and leadership and a variety of applied ethics issues and has also authored a number of chapters in books on related issues.

After retiring in the rank of Brigadier General in 1995, General Wakin served the Air Force Academy for another two years as the Lyon Chair Professor of Professional Ethics. He holds a Ph.D. in philosophy from the University of Southern California, an M.A. in secondary education and school administration from the State University of New York at Albany, and a B.A. in mathematics from the University of Notre Dame. He also was awarded honorary degrees by St. Mary's University (San Antonio) and Illinois Benedictine University. He was featured as one of twelve "great professors" in *People Magazine*, October 13, 1975, and was the subject of a feature article in the November 19, 1984 issue of *Newsweek*. General Wakin was national chairman of the Joint Services Conference on Professional Ethics from 1979 to 1992 and has been a member of the Ethics Oversight Committee for the U.S. Olympic Committee since 1991. He continues to average approximately fifty lectures each year to a variety of audiences around the world.